The Search for Lost Cities

The jungle-covered ruins of Angkor Wat: a city built not for men and commerce but to glorify god-kings during their life and after their death

JAMES WELLARD

The Search for Lost Cities

Constable London

First published in Great Britain 1980
by Constable and Company Limited
10 Orange Street London WC2H 7EG
Copyright © 1980 by James Wellard
Set in Monotype Fournier 12pt
Printed in Great Britain by The Anchor Press Ltd
and bound by Wm Brendon & Son Ltd
both of Tiptree, Essex

British Library Cataloguing in Publication Data

Wellard, James
     The search for lost cities.
     1. Cities and towns, ruined, extinct, etc.
     I. Title
     910'.09'1732   CC165

     ISBN 0-09-463140-9

Contents

Illustrations

Preface

This book is intended to have a practical, as well as an historical, use; and while it is realized that many, perhaps most, readers will never have the chance to visit in person all of the ten cities here described, it is hoped that their interest will have been stimulated sufficiently to encourage them to set off for some of the more easily reached places. All ten cities were until recently accessible by air, either direct to the sites themselves or to the nearest capital, from whence it was possible to finish the journey by road, with a rest-house for an overnight stay usually available.

Unfortunately the political instability of much of the world to-day can upset any plans we make to visit areas which for years have seemed safe for travel. Nobody seems able to predict nowadays what will happen in the Near, Middle, or Far East, or, for that matter, in South America. But making the possibly over-optimistic assumption that one day the current wars and upheavals will cease, thus enabling the tourist to go in safety from one country to another (as he could and did in the great days of Rome), the following are the itineraries for reaching the ten cities presented as a challenge to the more adventurous traveller.

I   SODOM AND GOMORRAH

Air to Amman, Jordan. Bus to Kerak. Taxi down to the Dead Sea.

2 MARIB
Air to Sa'ana, North Yemen. Air to Marib. Rest-house.

3 MOHENJO-DARO
Air to Karachi, Pakistan. Coach to the ruins. Rest-house.

4 ANGKOR
Air to Phnom Penh (Kampuchea). Air to Siem Reap. Local transport.

5 GARAMA
Air to Sebha (Fezzan) via Tripoli where arrangements would have to be made with a Travel Agency for the journey to Germa where a rest-house is available.

6 ZIMBABWE
Air to Salisbury, Rhodesia, where arrangements can be made to visit the Ruins in the National Park.

7 COPÁN
Air to Tegucigalpa (capital of Honduras). Special flight to Copán.

8 CITY OF RALEIGH
To Roanoke Island, North Carolina.

9 TARXIEN
Air to Malta. Local bus.

10 CALLEVA (Silchester)
To Reading by train or coach. Local bus.

Introduction

On one of my early travels in the Libyan Sahara, I nearly passed by an abandoned and nameless city which I would never have known had existed if my guide, a Tuareg camel-man, had not pointed it out. It was a rock-built city enclosed within a high wall buttressed with round turrets and pierced by a single gateway. It lay on the side of a stony escarpment and completely merged in with the landscape, which was why I had not noticed it. I stopped, of course, and spent a long afternoon exploring the narrow streets and wandering in and out of the houses which were constructed of lumps of rock fitted together without mortar. I was unable to find a single clue as to who had built this place, for there was nothing resembling a domestic artefact to be seen; nor was I able to discover much about it from the residents of the nearby oases, except that it was the largest of three similar deserted communities situated at intervals along the escarpment. The legend had it that these fortress-cities, which is what they obviously were, had been built by negroes, and this clue at least ties in with the pre-colonial history of the Sahara such as we know it. There were powerful negro kingdoms during the fourteenth and fifteenth centuries along the Niger River, and the armies of one of them, the Songhai, may have invaded this fertile valley which once formed the kingdom of the Garamantes.[1]

1. See Chapter 5.

My experience in the Fezzan goes to show that there are still corners of this teeming world where the modern traveller can share, if only in a modest manner, the personal thrill of those early explorers who first saw the magnificent lost cities of antiquity; and for me the story of their discovery is an essential part of the fascination of these places, all the more so as to-day we can reach most of them in safety and comfort. To this extent, one could say that something of their enchantment has been lost, and it is hoped that the journey we are about to take will restore a little of their magic.

It will be seen that I have not chosen the more obvious historic cities – Ur, Troy, Babylon, Petra, Palmyra, and so forth. I have tried instead to select examples which belong to the more obscure chapters of history and which, by the same token, tend to be off the well-beaten track. In addition, nearly all the places I have visited, then studied and thought about, have what might be called a certain philosophical significance, which is why I have begun the search with Sodom and Gomorrah. These Cities of the Plain hold a unique place in the story of civilization, because if we accept the Biblical account (and there is no other), they were destroyed not only by brimstone and fire, but by their perverseness in accepting a god who tolerated human sacrifice, temple prostitution, worship of serpents, and so forth. The practice of homosexuality, as we shall see, was merely incidental to their religion. Sodom and Gomorrah, then, were urban personifications, as it were, of the decadent Moabites against whom were ranged the stern, disciplined nomads of the desert; and the Hebrew scribes drew from the physical cataclysm which overwhelmed them the first and perhaps the most important moral lesson to be found in recorded history.

One could point to some such underlying theme in the ruin or abandonment of the other lost cities we are considering – Marib, the capital of the Kingdom of Sheba, for instance.

Does not Muhammad, who might well have visited the place with a caravan and certainly knew the circumstances of its destruction, state that its downfall was due in the final analysis to its wickedness?

> For the people of Saba turned away from the truth. So we afflicted them with a devastating flood and converted their fruitful gardens into gardens bearing bitter fruit . . .[1]

What the Prophet was saying was that the great dam at Marib,[2] one of the wonders of the world, did not collapse simply because of man's negligence, but because of God's wrath, an exact parallel with the Jewish explanation of the destruction of Sodom and Gomorrah. It was another lesson for the attention of future generations.

Rationalist historians have, of course, pooh-poohed this view of history and have put forward pretty well every reason for the decline and fall of nations except a spiritual one. The reasons given in our textbooks are various, depending upon the intellectual fashion of the time – economic, social, or political. Yet it must be obvious that all these factors, including religion, are interdependent and that where one of them fails to function, the whole machinery of society is weakened. It is therefore conceivable that the twilight period of every city we are to discuss showed the same pattern of degeneration: religious and moral values rejected; central authority weakened; the rule of law and order challenged; the older citizens disheartened and fearful; the younger cynical and heartless. Finally, total dissolution.

Whether this decay of cities and of the civilization they represented is an inevitable law of history is, of course, debatable, and it would be rash to jump to conclusions, although where there is a contemporary account of what life

1. *The Koran*, Sura 34.
2. See Chapter 2.

was actually like at the end of an era, we are in a better position to see the forces of change and decay at work. For example, the Frenchman[1] Rutilius Claudius Namatianus, who has been called the last of the pagan poets and who lived at a time when towns like the Romano-British Calleva Atrebatum was becoming abandoned, could have described the scene for us, as he described the end of the Roman world as seen from the ship which was sailing back to his homeland along the western coast of Italy. What his poem reveals is the same story of collapse that the Old Testament tells in the case of Sodom and the Koran in that of Marib: the springs of government were worn out all over the Roman world; religion, laws, military and civil discipline, the seat of jurisdiction in Rome, the coinage, even the language itself, had all been undermined and debased. It was a time when the Empire was being shaken by continual barbarian invasions and no civilized authority seemed to have the will to resist; and one senses that Rutilius's description of the ravaged landscape of his native Gaul could equally have referred to southern Britain where the cities, towns, forts, villas, roads, and the whole complex of a once prosperous and peaceful society were crumbling.

It is, however, obvious that without written records of the kind that Rutilius left us for the Roman Empire in the fifth century and the Venerable Bede for Britain in the eighth we shall never really know the details of the gradual decline and outright abandonment of the cities that we are to visit, not even in the case of the City of Raleigh which is as near to us in time as the Elizabethan Age. The story of such places is a mystery, and fact often more puzzling than theory, as we shall see when examining the ruins of Mohenjo-Daro, Copán, and Tarxien.

210 ; or 3 ll. 1. The term 'Frenchman' is used here as more expressive and certainly more convenient, than 'a Romanized native of gaul'. Elsewhere 'English', 'Irish', and 'Scottish' are occasionally substituted for the formal Latin names.

This book is largely the result of my travels, which have in many cases been journeys of exploration. What struck me most forcibly on the very earliest of my expeditions and what eventually led me to read the works of my predecessors was the strangeness of large and manifestly once populous cities standing in ruins in the middle of nowhere. Perhaps the most splendid of such deserted places are found in North Africa where cities like Lepcis Magna give the impression that, with some tidying up, they could again become living communities. Why, then, did they surrender so easily to the barbarians? What happened to the will of the citizens that they put up so little resistance to forces, internal as well as external, obviously determined to destroy them?

These are questions which the thoughtful traveller, whether standing in the midst of the ruins of Timgad in Algeria or of Verulamium in Britain, is bound to ask himself, the question that our greatest historian asked in the forum of imperial Rome, while 'musing amidst the ruins of the Capitol where the bare-footed friars were singing vespers in the temple of Jupiter'. And like Gibbon, some of those explorers who first crossed mountains and deserts to find such legendary cities as Marib and Angkor and Copán also asked the same questions, so eloquently intimated by John Lloyd Stephens after he had hacked his way through the jungle finally to gaze upon the ruins of a lost Mayan city.

> The city was desolate. It lay before us like a shattered bark in the midst of the ocean, her masts gone, her name effaced, her crew perished, and none to tell whence she came, to whom she belonged, or what caused her destruction.

It is in this spirit of a search rather than of an archaeological tour that I have tried to describe the following ten cities, two each in the five main historic areas of the world and each typifying the rise and fall of a vanished civilization.

I am indebted to many officials in many countries for assistance given me during my travels over the last thirty years and, above all, to the Superintendent and staff of the Reading Room of the British Museum for making available so many indispensable books which the reader who wishes to pursue his studies of these ancient places will find quoted or referred to in the Bibliography. Practically every one of the marvellous narratives of the great explorers is, alas! out of print and only obtainable now in the great national libraries.

Finally, again my thanks to Mrs Barbara Nelson-Smith who worked with me in the typing of the manuscript.

J.W.

Part 1
Asia – the Middle East

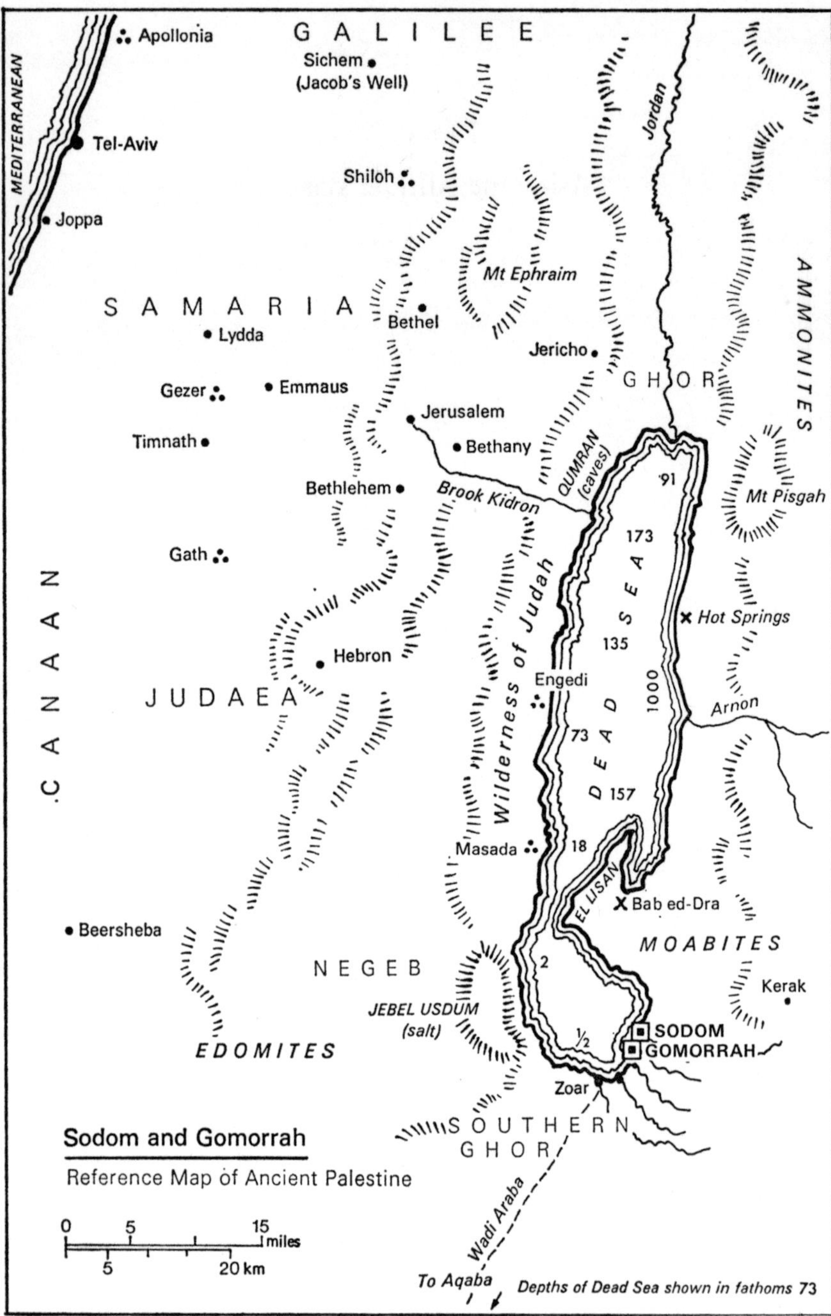

Sodom and Gomorrah

Reference Map of Ancient Palestine

Sodom and Gomorrah

You had best spend the night at the West Jordanian town of Kerak before going down to Sodom and Gomorrah. Situated on the heights overlooking the Dead Sea, it is a good place to begin the search, for the historians tell us that Kerak is the Kir Hareseth or Kir Heres of the Old Testament, a Moabite town which is related to the Cities of the Plain and, like them, has the distinction of being among the most hated and best cursed of places mentioned in the Old Testament. You will probably wonder why as you wander through the drab streets of modern Kir Hareseth, since the only evidence that the town has any historical significance is the ruin of the mighty Crusader's Castle, Le Crac du Désert, towering above the cluster of jerry-built houses typical of a twentieth-century provincial community in this part of the world. No signs at all, then, of that Moabite town upon which the old prophets, particularly that master of imprecations, Jeremiah, rained down maledictions. The cause of all this sound and fury was the obstinacy of its king, one Mesha, in resisting the Israelites' besieging army and, as a last resort, publicly sacrificing his son on the city walls. To a Moabite like King Mesha, the 'passing of a child (especially his own) through the fire' was a profoundly religious act. To the Jews it was a patent attempt at trickery.

The walls of Kir Hareseth have, of course, long since gone, and Le Crac du Désert is an empty ruin. Both came to an abrupt and terrible end: what was left of the Moabite citadel was razed to the ground by the builders of the Christian fortress which, in turn, was sacked by the Moslems. And standing on the ramparts of the Castle from which prisoners were thrown down the cliff with wooden boxes over their heads so as to prolong their suffering, one can only conclude that such a place deserved what it got.

But Kerak is where you stay before going down to the Plain. There is no hotel with modern conveniences, for the town no longer has its ancient importance as a fortress on the King's Highway which ran from Damascus to the Gulf of Aqaba, or as a pilgrims' caravanserai on the Baghdad to Mecca road. There aren't any pilgrim caravans crossing Jordan to-day, and you won't see a camel chewing the cud outside a shop selling the usual western trumperies. Most tourists wanting a quick look at the Crusaders' Castle arrive by taxi from Amman, the capital of Jordan, and return the same day. We remain and make our way to the rest-house built by the Jordanian government for the accommodation of the occasional student of history who chooses to linger in these parts. If the rest-house is full or closed for repairs, the traveller will be permitted to bed down inside the Great Hall of the Crusaders' Castle, provided he can find the guardian with the key to the fortress. A camp bed and sleeping-bag are recommended in this eventuality, for the cavernous Hall is dark, cold, and after heavy rains, slightly flooded. For those with strong imaginations it is also peopled with the ghosts of the soldiers and slaves who occupied the fortress for forty-six years between 1142 and 1188 when the Crusaders ruled the Kingdom of Oultre Jourdain, especially under that most formidable of medieval gangsters, the French knight Renaud de Chatillon. It was in this Great Hall that the survivors of a five-year siege made their last stand before being massacred by the army of Saladin; and here, too, seven hundred years later, that the first explorers of the Dead Sea made their headquarters. It is a fitting time to remember them; the Swiss traveller Burckhardt on his way to discover Petra; the English sailors Irby and Mangles, the first explorers of the Dead Sea Coast; the American naval lieutenant Lynch who charted the Sea itself; and all those Victorian scholars who rode up to this fortress with their escort of villainous tribesmen.

And so before we set off on our own exploration, we salute these now near-forgotten travellers from a city so ancient and ravaged by wars that it seems to encapsulate a landscape that has seen more conflict than any region of similar size in the world. For looking down from the Castle on to the Dead Sea, as they did, the observer has before him the microcosm, as it were, of religious wars from the time of Abraham to the present, for these wars and the national conflicts they have engendered are still with us to-day. There is scarcely a fold in the hills where some tumbled heap of stones, once some nation's stronghold, does not remind us of events which continue to affect the lives of us all, so that from a lofty pinnacle on the road down to the Dead Sea, one can glimpse not only Mount Pisgah from which Moses viewed the Promised Land, but Masada where his descendants lost it. And the traveller is well aware if he is on the Jordanian side of the sea that the struggle for the possession of this geologically fractured land still continues with as much bitterness as when the tribes of Abraham came out of the desert to the south in search of new pastures.

The Jews arrived at the Moabite frontier around 1900 BC, and we shall see when visiting the Plain why Abraham decided that this was the region where his tribesmen should settle. The region is still one of the most fruitful in Jordan, remarkably so in view of the aridity and desolation of the rest of the Dead Sea littoral. In the springtime it is so green with its fig, pomegranate, and olive trees that it is not difficult to see why it was likened in Genesis to 'the garden of the Lord'. Moreover, there is no doubt at all that Palestine was far more fertile in ancient times than it is to-day, for the deterioration and desiccation of the soil are not the result of a climatic change, but of the devastations of men.

But seen from the mountain overlooking the Dead Sea, the Plain below gives no indication of this ancient fertility, or that it once supported five small kingdoms which the Bible lists as Sodom, Gomorrah, Admah, Zeboiim and Zoar. There must have also been many Moabite towns and fortresses which controlled the most important communication route of the pre-classical world, notably the Incense Road which crossed Arabia to Petra and then ran north along the King's Highway to Babylon. Yet there were undoubtedly some remains of the Moabite kingdoms in classical times, for both the Greek geographer Strabo writing around AD 20 and the Roman historian Tacitus, pro-consul of Asia in AD 112, mention the ruins of several cities still visible on the Plain. Furthermore, some urban community still called Sodom was certainly on the map up to the middle of the fourth century, for a bishop of Sodom attended the First Council of Nicaea in AD 325.

Apart, however, from references in classical writers to the outer walls of the Cities of the Plain being still visible in their time, all material evidence of their existence seems to have disappeared by the Middle Ages, although these bywords of infamy remained something of a tourist attraction to the early pilgrims who came from all over Christendom to visit the shrines and monuments of the Bible lands. Most of the pilgrims accepted as gospel the destruction of Sodom and Gomorrah as an example of divine justice; but by the eighteenth century, historians had begun to question the doctrine that natural disasters like floods and earthquakes were caused by divine wrath.

Sceptics went even further. They argued that the Hebrew scribes had used the charge of pederasty against the Moabites to justify the Israelite invasion of another tribe's territory with a view to the occupation of the fertile lands of the Dead Sea coast. The truth of the matter, this argument went, was that all Semitic people have tolerated homosexuality at one stage or another in their history and that the rabbis' righteous indignation was actually motivated more by fear of the Moabite gods than by the abhorrence of their sexual practices. In other words, Chemosh of the Moabites, Ashtar of the Canaanites, Baal of the Philistines were deities who challenged the omnipotence of Yahweh and were therefore to be discredited by every means possible, along with their adherents. Was it not conceivable, then, that the whole story of the Cities of the Plain and their destruction by Yahweh was an invention designed to vindicate the aggression of the Chosen People? Were there such wicked cities as Sodom and Gomorrah? And if so, where was the factual evidence of their existence?

With a view to answering these questions, a succession of travellers set out at the beginning of the last century to explore what had become one of the least known regions of the world: namely, Judaea and the Land of Moab. It was, after all, in these lands that history began for devout Christians; here that the seeds of Western religion were sown; and here that the author of that religion once lived. But since the Crusades the whole area had been closed off by the Arabs to the infidel, and the lawlessness of the Bedouin tribes made it doubly dangerous to explorers. That was why few travellers had ever reached the southern shores of the Dead Sea and none had actually sailed on its waters.

The first to reach the Land of Moab was a German traveller, Ulrich Jasper Seetzen, the son of a farmer, who set off in 1802 for Palestine where, disguised as a beggar, he wandered around the Dead Sea in search of the countries and cities mentioned in the Bible. Seetzen was certainly the first modern traveller to have reached the Land of Moab where he learnt from his Arab guides that the remains of ancient buildings were still to be found beneath the waters of the Buhayrat Lut, as they called the Dead Sea. But he was only able to spend a single day on the southern shore where he discovered what he thought was the Zoar of the Bible, and so provided the first clue to the historians who were now trying to decide whether Sodom and Gomorrah were situated to the north or to the south of the Dead Sea. Seetzen then continued his journey by way of Sinai to Egypt whence he travelled in the disguise of a pilgrim to Mecca which he reached in 1809, forty-four years before Richard Burton's famous *hadj*. He made extensive journeys in Arabia, finally disappearing altogether somewhere on the road to San'a in North Yemen. He may have been murdered by bandits or have died from the 'fever'. He was forty-three years old.

What Seetzen had done with his announcement of the discovery of Zoar, one of the five Cities of the Plain, was to stimulate the interest of both scholars and laymen in the story of Sodom and Gomorrah, an interest which continued and increased throughout the nineteenth and early decades of the twentieth century. The finding of the city which was spared in order to accommodate Lot was accepted as proof of the literal truth of the Bible. The next step was to locate the sites of the other four cities, which meant making decisions on the basis of what clues the Old Testament provided. The arguments now centred on the question as to whether the Moabite settlements were situated to the north of the Dead Sea, to the south, or beneath its waters. The controversy was quite lively, and, as one would expect, the German savants were especially dogmatic on the matter. Obviously some sound scientific exploration was required, in particular a charting of the Dead Sea itself and the plains, or *ghors* as they were called, at each end of it.

A hydrographical survey of the Sea had actually been undertaken in 1847 by a British naval officer, Lieutenant William Molyneux of HMS *Spartan*. Molyneux had been commissioned by the Admiralty to command a small expedition 'to examine the course of the River Jordan . . . and especially to measure the depth of the Dead Sea'.[1] He was to be accompanied by three 'good volunteer seamen from the ship and a dragoman called Toby'. Horses and camels were provided by the vice-consul at Acre, the camels to carry a small boat in which the team intended to sail down the Jordan and circumnavigate the Dead Sea.

Obviously Molyneux was a better sailor than he was explorer, and consequently he often found himself unable to cope with the Bedouin tribesmen who made their usual exorbitant demands for safe-conduct through their territories. In short, he tended to alienate these fierce Palestinians who made his journey down the Jordan as difficult as they could.

Soon afterwards [he writes] they wanted me to pay for corn for their horses, which I again refused, and again there was a row. I had bother enough to-day to drive any reasonable person mad: almost every minute of it I was expecting that we should come to blows, but happily I had several barrels [pistols] about my person.[2]

It comes as no surprise to us, then, that Molyneux 'was a good deal knocked up by the sun to-day'; and getting down to the Dead Sea was almost like moving an army in an enemy's country; and, finally, that his sailors taking the boat down the river while he followed on land were ambushed, stripped of their arms and ammunition, robbed of their hats, and driven

1. Lieutenant William Molyneux, 'Expedition to the Jordan and Dead Sea', *Journal of the Royal Geographical Society*, Vol 18 (1848), p 104 ff.
2. *op cit*, p 113.

off into the hills. Now Molyneux had no idea where his men were, whether alive or dead, and he was in serious trouble.

> For two or three hours in misery and distress of mind, silently and in the dark (for the moon was not yet up) we wound about the ravines and bushes, in vain calling out the names of our lost friends ... My horse fell down the side of a hill; the guides, camels, and mules tumbled by turns; every moment we expected a crowd of ruffians to rush upon us ...
>
> We were now nearly in the centre of the ghor, surrounded by tribes of the greatest possible rogues, in despair of finding our poor people, and the moon just rising above the hills.[1]

Lieutenant Molyneux never did find his men until he returned to his ship two weeks later and discovered them safe and sound on board the HMS *Spartan*. They had simply set out on foot for the Mediterranean coast after the attack by the Arabs, a journey of some sixty miles, and the fact that they carried no arms (the absence of their hats was of no significance) was probably in their favour in the view of the tribesmen through whose territory they passed, for a true believer is not supposed to harm a woman, Jew, or unarmed traveller. Molyneux, in the meantime, no doubt hardly daring to report back to his captain that he had accomplished precisely nothing for the loss of three good seamen, decided to make a quick survey of the Dead Sea which he was able to reach with his boat on Saturday 4 September 1847. He now took a few bearings and soundings which added something to the general knowledge of the area, the most important fact being the discovery of the great depth of the Dead Sea in the northern section. Molyneux

1. *op cit*, p 122.

reports that his lead went down 225 fathoms (1,350 feet) without his being convinced that it had touched bottom. Unfortunately, because of the heat and hazards of the undertaking, he was unable to get his boat into the waters south of the El Lisan peninsula. By this time 'We were all completely knocked up,' he writes, 'and the sea also got up so rapidly that the little boat took in much water, and we began to think that we should first be thrown overboard, for she was too deep.'[1]

In short, Lieutenant Molyneux abandoned his project of charting the Dead Sea and so missed discovering the most important fact of all about it, a fact which is extremely relevant to the destruction of the Cities of the Plain. But the world had not long to wait for this vital information; still another sailor, this time an American, was heading for Palestine and the Dead Sea at the very time the English officer had decided to leave the hated place. It is not difficult to see why. He had lost three of his crew; he himself was worn out with his constant ordeals; and, to crown it all, his boat was now practically useless, 'covered with a nasty slimy substance . . . iron dreadfully corroded . . . constant thirst and drowsiness . . . no appetite . . .'[2]

Lieutenant William Francis Lynch sailed from New York aboard the US store ship *Supply* on 26 November 1847. He had been commissioned by the Hon J. Y. Mason, Secretary of the Navy 'to explore a distant river [the Jordan] and its wondrous reservoir [the Dead Sea] – the first teeming with sacred associations and the last enveloped in a mystery which has defied all previous attempts to penetrate it'.[3] His party was composed

1. *op cit*, p 128.
2. *ibid.*
3. W. F. Lynch, *Narrative of the Expedition to the River Jordan and the Red Sea*, London; Blackwood, 1855. p v.

of two other officers, one a cartographer, the other a botanist, and ten ordinary seamen of whom the lieutenant writes:

> I was very particular to select young, native-born Americans, of sober habits, from each of whom I exacted a pledge to abstain from all intoxicating drinks.[1]

Lynch also took with him two metal boats, one of copper, the *Fanny Mason*, and one of galvanized iron, the *Fanny Skinner*, named after the daughters of the patrons of the expedition. The lieutenant's earnest hope (he writes) was that the two *Fannies* would sustain him 'whether threading the rapids of the Jordan, or floating on the wondrous sea of death'. Also part of his equipment was enough fire-power to demonstrate American determination not to be deterred by either the lawlessness or the rapacity of the tribes: weapons included a blunderbuss (a short, bell-muzzled gun meant for shooting at close quarters); fourteen carbines with long bayonets; fourteen pistols – four of them revolvers and ten with bowie-knives attached; ammunition belts; and a sword for each of the officers.

The expedition was undoubtedly a model of organization in the best tradition of the US Navy, and Lieutenant Lynch's narrative, written on his return home a year later (and written, as he tells us, in haste on his learning that another and unauthorized member of the expedition was preparing to forestall him), a good example of nineteenth-century travel literature. It is difficult for us to-day, when the Dead Sea is lined with hotels and holiday camps, to realize how wild and hazardous this area was only 133 years ago; and we read with something like amazement how the lieutenant and his crew launched their little boat in the teeth of a gale, to be driven back by the northeast wind far from the shore, prompting Lieutenant

1. *op cit*, p 13.

Lynch to write: 'There is a tradition among the Arabs that no one can venture upon this sea and live.' However, the sailors survived this ordeal and came safely to shore in the darkness.

Lynch spent three weeks charting the Dead Sea, from the northern coast where the Sea receives the river Jordan to the marshlands at the southern end. His plan was to criss-cross the lake diagonally, sounding as he went and making observations on the geography, geology, and history of the area. His is the first naval chart of this inland sea, and he was the first to discover its most significant feature: namely, the great disparity between the depths of the northern and southern basins. It was this factor which was eventually to provide the clue to what might actually have happened in the time of Abraham, a clue which would, in turn, help solve the controversy as to the whereabouts of the five Cities of the Plain. In fact, Lieutenant Lynch himself believed that he had identified the probable location of Sodom and Gomorrah by revealing that the northern basin of the Dead Sea had an average depth of 217 fathoms, or 1,302 feet, whereas the lake south of the tongue of land called el Lisan averaged only two fathoms or twelve feet. This extraordinary difference in the levels of the sea-bed suggested that the southern basin had once been dry land which had been flooded *following an earthquake*, a cataclysm evidently accompanied by emissions of ignited sulphur – the brimstone and fire of the Bible. The American officer's exploration, in fact, was the forerunner of all subsequent geological and hydrological surveys of the rift valley which extends from Lake Tiberias to the junction of the Gulf of Aqaba and the Red Sea; and as a result of these surveys, geologists are now agreed that Lynch was correct in siting Sodom and Gomorrah south of el Lisan.

Lynch, therefore, was not exaggerating his achievement when he wrote in his log under the date Tuesday 9 May [1848]:

The exploration of this sea was now complete; we had carefully sounded its depths, determined its geographical position, taken topographical sketches of its shores . . . and noted the winds, currents, changes of weather and all atmospheric phenomena.[1]

He could have added that he was also the first modern traveller to have seen the famous Pillar of Salt, of which he gives a precise description as to its height and bulk, an illustration in his book, and this summary of his impressions:

We immediately pulled in for the shore, and Dr. Anderson and I went up to examine it . . . We found the pillar to be of solid salt, capped with carbonate of lime, cylindrical in front and pyramidal behind. The upper or rounded part is about forty feet high, resting on a kind of oval pedestal from forty to sixty feet above the level of the sea. It slightly decreases in size upwards, crumbles at the top, and is one entire mass of crystallization. A prop, or buttress, connects it with the mountain behind. Its peculiar shape is doubtless attributable to the action of the winter rains . . .

It was a scene of unmitigated desolation. On one side rugged and worn, was the salt mountain of Usdum, with its conspicuous pillar which reminded us at least of the catastrophe of the plain; on the other were the lofty and barren cliffs of Moab, in one of the caves of which the fugitive Lot found shelter. To the south was an extensive flat with the high hills of Edom semi-girdling the salt plain where the Israelites repeatedly overthrew their enemies; and to the north was the calm and motionless sea, curtained with a purple mist,

1. Official Report . . . by Lieut W. F. Lynch, USN, Baltimore: Printed by John Murphy, 1852, p 42.

while deep in the slimy mud lay embedded the ruins of the ill-fated cities of Sodom and Gomorrah.[1]

Lieutenant Lynch's conclusions as to the site of Sodom and Gomorrah were reached after he had completed his circumnavigation of the Dead Sea and were shared by even those of his companions who had started out on the journey extremely sceptical of what he calls 'the Mosaic account', but who 'after twenty-two days of close investigation, were unanimously convinced of the truth of the Scriptural account of the destruction of the Cities of the Plain'.[2]

Such a conclusion from an explorer of the actual region was of great importance at a time when scientists were questioning the historicity of the Old Testament – in particular, the Book of Genesis. The Lynch expedition, in fact, could be said to have introduced a whole new era in Biblical scholarship. Exploration of the Holy Land was now to be liberally financed by American millionaire philanthropists; and by the end of the century the wandering scholar was to be superseded by the specialist. Moreover, the region where travellers like the American professor Edward Robinson of New York and the English canon, H. B. Tristram of Durham, had marched with a small caravan were soon to be surveyed by army engineers (the future Lord Kitchener among them) and to a considerable extent civilized. It was now the turn of the professional historians and archaeologists to pronounce on the truth of the story of Sodom and Gomorrah, and their verdict, based on the findings not only of their colleagues, but also of geographers

1. *Narrative, op cit*, p 310. One of Lynch's party, however, gives somewhat different dimensions for this salt pillar, stating that it was over sixty feet in height with a circumference of forty-five feet. This sailor seems to have been more of a sceptic than his commander, for he adds, 'it is hard to believe that Lot's wife was so large a person'.
2. *Narrative, op cit*, p 380.

and geologists, is conclusive: the young American naval lieutenant and his twelve shipmates were right: Sodom and Gomorrah lie under the shallow waters in the southern section of the Dead Sea, still overlooked by the Pillar of Salt.

Even so, despite the reports of aviators who claim to have discerned ruins beneath the surface (the 'shadows' that the Jewish historian Josephus refers to?), nobody has yet undertaken the necessary subaquatic exploration of the Dead Sea's southern embayment; and the most significant evidence that we have so far is found in the ruins of a Bronze Age settlement on a hill to the east of the Lisan peninsula. These are the extensive ruins first noticed by Captains Irby and Mangles during their expedition of 1818, later to be spotted by the Duc de Luynes who did not, however, get off his horse to examine them. Bab ed-Dra, as the settlement is called, was not excavated until the mid-1920s when the French archaeologist, Father Alexis Mallon SJ, with Professor William Albright, Director of the American School of Oriental Research at Jerusalem, made the most important discovery of all in the century-long search for Sodom and Gomorrah. In 1924 Father Mallon began to excavate a great fortress at Bab ed-Dra with 12-foot thick and 15-foot high walls encircling a settlement whose sherds dated from 2300–1900 BC – that is, from the time of Abraham. And just as significant as this dating of Bab ed-Dra was the discovery of seven fallen monoliths, identified as sacred cult pillars, which had been erected close to a necropolis, presumably the burial ground for royal personages from the kingdoms in the Plain below. The tombs, which were circular and built of dressed stones, still contained a few pieces of pottery and human remains which crumbled into dust on being touched. Any other objects they may have contained – ornaments, weapons, utensils, and so forth – had long since disappeared, purloined by ancient tomb robbers.

The existence at Bab ed-Dra of a citadel, an open-air

Lt Lynch, USN, first circumnavigator of the Dead Sea, discovers 'Lot's wife', the pillar of salt at Usdum, near the drowned cities of Sodom and Gomorrah

One of the two towers of the
Great Dam of Marib, a huge
and sophisticated construction
built about the ninth century
BC to irrigate tens of thousands
of acres of desert

Stones carved with Himyarite
inscriptions still abound among
the sand-dunes and the rubble
of Marib today

sanctuary of sacred monoliths, a necropolis, and a settlement for resident priests and visiting pilgrims is proof that an ancient civilization flourished on the southern shores of the Dead Sea precisely at the time Lot decided to move his tents to Sodom. And once his tribe had settled down in the Plain, it is probable that the Israelites visited Bab ed-Dra and frequented the religious festivals and country fairs that took place there. Fraternization of the Chosen People with an alien race and their hated gods was bound to inspire later leaders in times of crisis to depict Sodom and Gomorrah as the epitomes of vice and Lot's wife as the warning of what happened to those who looked back with interest towards such centres of wickedness. Amos, Isaiah, Jeremiah, Ezekiel, Zephaniah, Peter, Paul, and Jude, all rail against these cities because their people had been in danger of becoming contaminated by a foreign creed and the practices that went with it.

But theological implications apart, it is evident that the discovery of the Bronze Age settlement at Bab ed-Dra provides an important clue to what may have happened in the second millennium BC when this Dead Sea civilization was wiped out. It is especially significant, for instance, that this Moabite sanctuary was not destroyed by war, which was the usual fate of protohistoric towns in this, the most fought-over region in the world. Instead, Bab ed-Dra appears to have been suddenly abandoned around 1900 BC which corresponds with the date of the destruction of the cities in the Plain below. The sanctuary must have survived the cataclysm because it was above the level of the flood waters which burst into the southern basin of the Dead Sea from the main area. The tombs built around the sacred precincts show no signs of inundation. The fallen monoliths which marked the High Place must have been toppled by the earth tremor which preceded the flood If, therefore ,we translate the somewhat lurid description or Genesis into geological language, we can postulate a catastrophic natural disaster resulting from a severe earthquake along one of the most unstable valleys in the world – the enormous rift which runs from Syria south by way of the river Jordan and the Dead Sea to the Gulf of Aqaba and so across the Red Sea through East Africa to Mozambique. This earthquake was followed by a conflagration caused by the ignition of gases and the seepage of oily substances from the wells of Siddim. The final catastrophe was the bursting of the waters through the barrier of the Lisan peninsula and the inundation of the whole shallow area we call the southern basin of the Dead Sea. If this hypothesis is correct, Sodom and Gomorrah lie submerged somewhere within this 200 square miles of marshland, and it will obviously need the new techniques and skills of marine archaeology to locate them.

Where, then, can we start the search?

First, we can safely assume that the Cities of the Plain, like any other Bronze Age settlements, must have been built on a fertile and, above all, a well-watered site. The southern end of the Dead Sea is rich in such sites, with good soil and five streams coming down from the mountains of Moab. Each of these streams has a sufficient perennial flow to support a town of several thousand people; and on this basis we can tentatively locate the five Cities on the banks of the five streams (see map). Sodom, which seems to have been the most important of them, for it is always mentioned first, would then be on the lowest reaches of the most abundant stream, the Seil en-Numeirah which still flows into the southern embayment of the Dead Sea. Gomorrah was, perhaps, on the banks of the Seil Esal to the south, and Zoar on the Seil el-Qurahi, or River Zered, not far from the Zoara of the classical period and the Segor of the Middle Ages. Admah and Zeboiim may be located on the remaining two streams.

True, there is nothing tangible to help us, no column, not even the vestiges of a wall projecting above the slate-grey surface of those still and ominous waters. Perhaps that is why the very air seems to be heavy with mystery. And standing on this shore at night, a traveller, even to-day when the tribes no longer wander through this land as they did until a mere fifty years ago, can still imagine the hillsides covered with the tents of Lot and the lights of Sodom and Gomorrah glimmering in the distance and up in the hills the fires smoking on the sacrificial altars of Bab ed-Dra. And it was perhaps on such a night that the earth moved, the very mountains trembled, emissions of sulphurous gas were ignited, and suddenly the waters of the Sea poured down from the north, and all the towns and villages with their fields and groves were inundated. Yahweh, enthroned on his ark and surrounded by his cherubim, had once again proved that he was a greater man of war than Chemosh of the Moabites. The Jewish tribes with their flocks and herds passed safely across the mountains of Moab *en route* to the Promised Land.

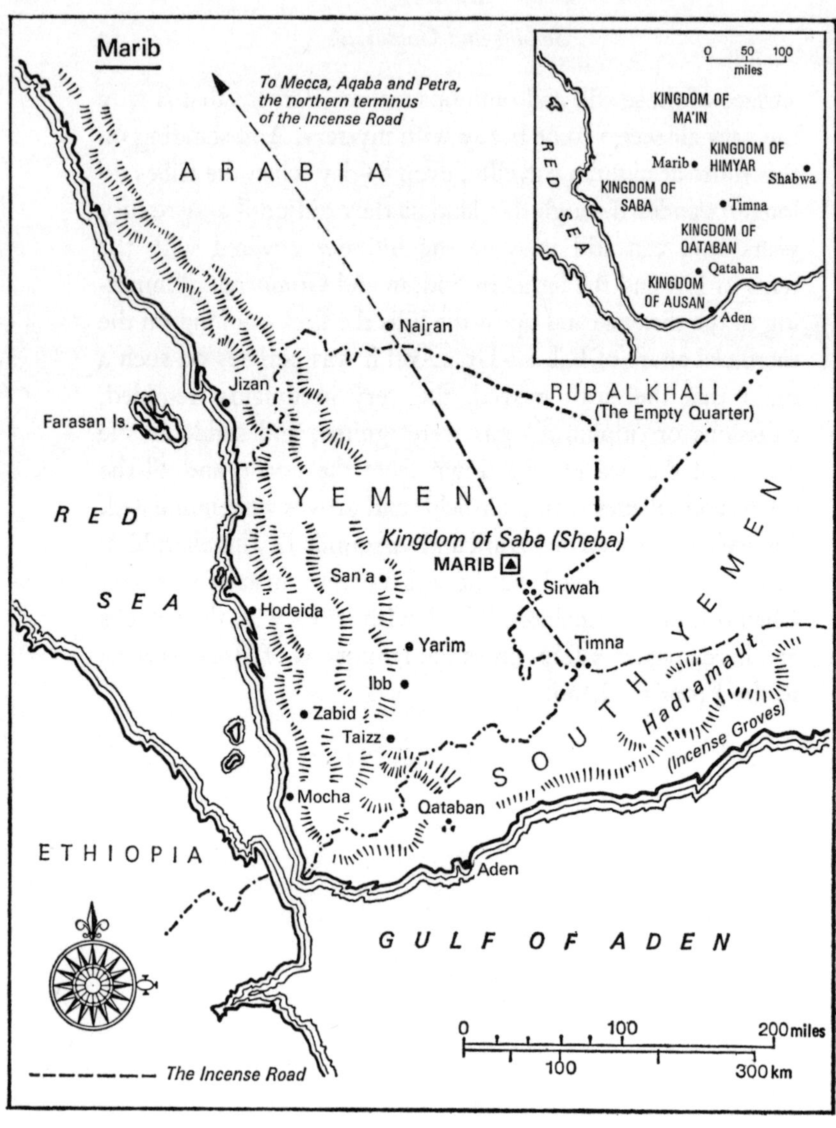

Marib
To Mecca, Aqaba and Petra, the northern terminus of the Incense Road
ARABIA
0 50 100 miles
KINGDOM OF MA'IN
KINGDOM OF HIMYAR
Marib
Shabwa
KINGDOM OF SABA
Timna
KINGDOM OF QATABAN
RED SEA
Qataban
KINGDOM OF AUSAN
Aden
Najran
Jizan
Farasan Is.
RUB AL KHALI
(The Empty Quarter)
YEMEN
RED
SEA
Kingdom of Saba (Sheba)
San'a
MARIB
Sirwah
Hodeida
Timna
SOUTH YEMEN
Yarim
Hadramaut
Ibb
(Incense Groves)
Zabid
Taizz
Mocha
Qataban
ETHIOPIA
Aden
GULF OF ADEN
0 100 200 miles
100 300 km
The Incense Road

Marib

To-day you can get to Marib fairly easily by air, but only with difficulty, if at all, by land. The official explanation is simple: it is called 'the unsettled state of the tribes'. In plain language, the unescorted traveller is liable to be ambushed and robbed between San'a, the modern capital of the Yemen, and Marib, the ancient capital of Saba, the Sheba of the Bible.

Nowadays a Dakota aeroplane, that old workhorse of the skies, is laid on to ferry tourists across the mountains to a country which is no longer on the map. It is, of course, the Arabia Felix of the Romans, or the al-Jumhuriyah al Arabiyah of the medieval Arab historians – to-day a region of the Yemen Arab Republic, a newly created state which is not that easy to find on the map, either.

Ten years ago, it was only the more enterprising traveller who got as far as San'a, a typical Middle Eastern city, half built of mud and bricks, half of dirty concrete, with precious little left to prove its claim to be the oldest inhabited metropolis in the world. For up to the time the Americans, Chinese, and Russians began to bid against each other for the privilege of building at their own expense roads, harbours, and airports for a country which had no evident wish to modernize itself, communications both with the outside world and within North Yemen were more primitive than they had been when the Queen of Sheba set out along the Incense Road to Jerusalem. Thirty years ago, for instance, a British mission was denied entrance into San'a because it was eight o'clock in the evening and the city gates were shut tight. But with the blessing of the Great Powers, progress has reached the Yemen: most of the city walls dating from the twelfth century have been bull-dozed down; many of the beautiful old houses destroyed; and jerry-built hotels of astonishing discomfort erected in their place. The land which for 2,000 years remained as mysterious as Plato's Atlantis is ready to receive the package-tourists.

The Dakota of the Yemeni Airways is about to take off – that is, if the pilot has not been allocated to another internal flight. There is also always the possibility in these newly created 'democracies' that a local politician will have commandeered the only available aircraft for a jaunt somewhere of his own. But eventually, when everybody who can argue his way on board is settled in the seats or on the floor, the plane lumbers up and away over the first foothills and through the mountain passes to the landing strip at Marib, where a runway in the sand, a hut, a pile of oil barrels, and a squad of unshaven soldiers armed with Russian machine-pistols await our arrival. One must admit that flying of this sort is much more enter-taining than it is on the international air routes; and for those who have read the narratives of the first Europeans to reach Marib, it is, more than that, an appropriate way of getting to this lost city which was once more splendid than Athens or Rome – a city of palaces and temples when London was a fisherman's village of wattles and reeds. Let us salute, then, the first explorers of Marib – Thomas Arnaud, Frenchman; Joseph Halévy, Jew; and Eduard Glaser, Austrian – as we climb from the aeroplane, for up to a few years ago, they were the only Europeans to have reached the Land of Sheba since the Roman general Aelius Gallus besieged Marib in 16 BC, only to withdraw, defeated by the terrain, with the loss of most of his army.

The struggle to discover this mysterious city, as we shall see, became intensified during that great age of exploration, the nineteenth century, when nearly every corner of the earth was being surveyed by explorers; and the determination to unravel the secrets of Sheba carried over to our own century and inspired men like André Malraux to attempt an aerial survey over the Eastern Yemen in 1934 when he was prohibited from travelling across the province by land. Without proper maps and a precise idea of what he was looking for, Malraux's efforts were fruitless: it is doubtful whether he saw Marib at all, even from the air. Nor, for that matter, did the most distinguished of modern explorers of the Arabian peninsula ever set foot inside the fabled city. H. St John Philby set out in 1936 with an expeditionary force of two motor cars, a supply caravan of twenty-five camels, and an escort of twenty-four Arabs representing the tribes he expected to meet along the way. Yet despite this small army, Philby was obliged to make his plans to visit Marib in secret, not even daring to let his escorts know where he was going. In fact, the explorer was unable to get nearer than five miles to Marib, even though he saw not a soul to stop him on that whole deserted plain. In the end, standing on the peak of an extinct volcanic cone, he had to be satisfied with just a glimpse of the fabled capital.

> I saw it through my glasses [he writes] as a group of buildings occupying the slopes and summit of a hill and forming a fine silhouette against the dull background of the plain beyond.[1]

What Philby saw was, of course, the half-ruined houses of medieval Marib, the tall, elongated buildings with their win-

1. H. St John Philby, 'The Land of Sheba', *The Geographical Journal*, Vol xcii, No 2 (August 1938), p 126.

dows outlined in white and their little screened balconies overhanging the street, an architecture which is unique to South Arabia. The Yemen is so primitive in all respects that the visitor is bound to be astonished at the elegance of these buildings and, even more, at the skill required to perch them atop the pinnacles of precipitous mountains, a common sight throughout the land. Indeed, one might go so far as to say that this architechtonic skill and aesthetic sense are the only discernible links between the Yemeni of to-day and their Himyarite ancestors who erected the temples, palaces, and vast irrigation works of the five kingdoms of Arabia Felix. These kingdoms had sprung up along the Incense Road, the most important highway of the ancient world from the time of Sumer to the end of the Roman empire, a duration of 3,500 years. The principal commerce of this road was the frankincense harvested in the groves of the Hadramaut and transported by caravans across the kingdoms of Qataban, Saba, and Ma'in, enriching these states as well as their neighbours, Ausan and Himyar, until they became the wealthiest regions in the Middle East. And this is why the Queen of Sheba could take as gifts to King Solomon 120 talents of gold (i.e., over four tons) and 'of spices a very great store, and precious stones: there came no more such abundance of spices as these which the Queen of Sheba gave to King Solomon.'[1]

But we may as well dispose of the legend of this Queen so dearly beloved of romance and especially of Arabian mythology in which she is known as Bilqis, for Sheba never did have a queen. The kingdom was ruled over by priest-kings from its beginnings around 950 BC until its conquest by the Abyssinians in the sixth century AD. Its rise and fall were, therefore, roughly contemporaneous with those of Rome, though here, of course, all resemblance ends. The Sabaeans were a trading

1. I Kings, 8:10.

people who supplied the whole of the ancient world as middle-men for the spices of the East and especially frankincense. It was, indeed, this latter product, grown only in southern Arabia and on the coast of Somalia, which accounted for the very existence, let alone the wealth of Saba and the other four kingdoms. For frankincense was burnt in enormous quantities in temples from Babylon to Carthage, fifty-eight tons of it consumed at one sacrificial rite in the temple of Bel, according to Herodotus, and the entire annual crop of Arabia at Poppaea's funeral in AD 66, according to Pliny the Elder.

All the classical historians and geographers were familiar with the name and general location of the South Arabian kingdoms, but no Greek or Roman seems to have visited Marib. Consequently the Western world knew very little about the Sabaeans themselves, except that they were rich and prosperous, were ruled over by kings, and worshipped the sun, moon, and stars. But was all this talk of their wealth exaggerated, like so many of the myths which grew up about those cities and nations which neither the armies nor the traders nor the explorers of the West were able to reach?

The traveller who manages to arrive at such places to-day – Timbuctoo in Mali, Balkh in Afghanistan, Sijilmassa in Morocco – will be disappointed if he expects to see such tangible evidence of wealth as the noble ruins left by the Greek and Roman builders. Marib is another 'golden city' of the imagination. From the aeroplane which drifts down to the plain below, the passenger will see only a stony desert, with no signs of life at all; and the pilot has alas! no time to fly over the great dam to show us the irrigation system which 3,000 years ago turned thousands of acres of now barren land into orchards and fields of grain. Only after landing will the visitor glimpse what is left of the capital of the kingdom of Saba, a walled city standing half-ruined on a hillock. And even when he actually enters through the town gate into the deserted streets, he will see nothing of the Mariaba of the Greek geographer Agatharchides who had heard reports from travellers of magnificent palaces in which the kings and nobles sat on couches overlaid with silver, drinking from golden goblets studded with gems. Such was the legendary wealth of this kingdom of Saba whose capital has been reduced to heaps of rubble where a few scraggy hens and a donkey or two search in the dust for a morsel of food. You will see no vestiges of the magnificent palaces, but only shuttered buildings, though if you look closer at the massive walls, you may spot a marble plaque on which is carved a Himyarite inscription, or a frieze of horned beasts carved on a slab of dressed stone.

There is something else. Choosing your time discreetly, visit the town mosque which is not easily spotted by those who associate Moslem places of worship with slender minarets and blue-tiled domes. The Marib mosque is just outside the main gate and at first glance looks like a stone-mason's shed, so full is it of pillars and shafts of every shape and size. What one is seeing, of course, are the columns of the Sabaean capital which were found half-sticking out of the ground and were used to support the roof of the mosque, just as Greek, Roman, and Byzantine pillars were used all over the Islamic world. The striking feature of the Marib mosque, though, is the number of pillars, so that the interior resembles a veritable forest.

The tall houses of the town itself have also been partially built from stone blocks, obviously taken from the ruins of Mariaba. The façades of these houses are white-washed and the windows filled with thin sheets of alabaster. Queer little observation platforms project from the upper floors of these houses, and if the visitor to Marib sees any occupant at all, it will be a woman peering down from these platforms, perhaps through the lattice-work which encloses them.

The tourist to Marib to-day is obliged to stay in the town's only lodging-house, the great five-storey tower just inside the gate. He will have an opportunity now to see the inside of a typical Yemeni house, a place built like a fortress, its one entrance closed by an iron-studded door which will be locked *from the outside* at night, so keeping the tourists in and the bandits out – a bizarre illustration of what they mean by the phrase, 'the unsettled state of the tribes'. The guest must climb to the topmost room by stone steps which for some inexplicable reason become steeper the higher one goes. In the end, hands as well as feet are required as in rock-climbing. But the living-room where one finally arrives is worth the physical struggle to get there. It has white walls with a beamed ceiling and traceried windows of stained glass which throw pretty golden and ruby lights on to the carpets. All round the room are bright cushions against which one can recline in an ambience of extraordinary restfulness. Here, too, at the top of this tower, one can gaze out towards the Plain of Saba (Ramlet Sabatein), and, far beyond the horizon, the mountains of Hadramaut with their frankincense groves, a landscape which has only been superficially explored and, for that matter, seen by no more than a handful of European travellers.

The Arabian peninsula has always been virtually closed to Western explorers, and actually still makes a pretty successful attempt to remain so, despite the need for expertise in the oil fields and the presence of American and European advisers. But the real proof of the Arab hostility to the West can be quickly demonstrated by any woman traveller who applies for a visa to visit Saudi Arabia, as a tourist or in any other capacity. She will be refused. She is, in a sense, the victim of the Saudis' vexation in having had to admit so many of the infidel into the territory of the Prophet. It is this historical and geographical fact of Muhammad's birthplace which has made

Arabia the last country of the Middle East to be explored, while it has made the Yemen the most dangerous, as Carsten Niebuhr, the German traveller and first European to get within even reach of Marib, was to discover.

Sponsored by King Frederick V of Denmark, Niebuhr led an expedition of four Danish scholars to the Arabian peninsula in 1763. The sole survivor of a seven-year exploration of Egypt, Sinai, the Yemen, Palestine, and Persia, he gave the world in his *Description of Arabia* the first factual account of the Yemen. But Niebuhr had had to pay a terrible price for his attempt to explore regions so hostile to Christians on physical as well as religious grounds. Before the expedition had been five months in the Yemen, Frederick von Haven, the Arabist, had died in Mocha where he was buried in the European cemetery, English sailors acting as his pall-bearers. Two months later, the expedition botanist Peter Forskäl was a victim of 'the fever', dying on the road to San'a, and presenting Niebuhr with still another instance of the dangers and difficulties of travel in a fanatical province of the world of Islam.

> Our greatest difficulty [he writes] was to find persons to bear the body to the grave; and this even though we promised to pay very liberally for the service. At last we prevailed with six men to convey it to the burying-place at midnight. They performed the task, but ran and hid themselves, in the best manner they could; so great is the aversion of those people to touch a Christian ... At Sana we learned that Mr. Forskell's body had been taken up by night, and that his grave clothes had been snatched away after the coffin was opened. The Dola [governor] obliged the Jews to bury it again, and left them the coffin for their pains.[1]

1. C. Niebuhr, *Travels through Arabia*, translated by Robert Heron, Edinburgh: Printed for R. Morisen, 1972, Vol I, p 360.

No other European seems to have travelled in the Yemen until the summer of 1836 when an English naval officer, Charles Cruttenden of the survey ship *Palinurus*, journeyed from Mocha to San'a in the hope of setting out from that town to Marib. In fact, Cruttenden might have been the first explorer to reach the Sabaean capital, had he not been prevented at the last minute by the Imam of San'a, Ali Mansur, whom the sailor describes as 'much addicted to drinking spirits and rarely sober after midday'. At any rate, this 'young man born of a Nubian mother and with a peculiarly disagreeable expression of countenance owing to a cast in his right eye' was convinced that Cruttenden and his companion Dr Hulton (who was soon after to die of the usual 'fever' which seems to have been a particularly virulent form of malaria) were spies and treasure-hunters and thereupon held them prisoners inside the palace compound. Cruttenden, then, never reached the mysterious lost city, but he did manage to copy four Himyarite inscriptions on stone slabs brought to San'a from Marib itself.

The largest of these stones and the one with the longest inscription was a slab of marble used to cover a hole in the roof of a mosque. On getting news of this treasure, Cruttenden set about bribing an attendant at the mosque to bring this slab to his lodgings at night. The bribing, of course, was easy. The difficult part of the operation was transporting the heavy stone from the mosque to the Imam's palace. One can imagine the scene – the 'borrowers' lowering the stone from the roof of the mosque and thus risking death at the hands of fanatics if caught; then the rush through the dark alleys back to the palace gardens where Cruttenden and Dr Hulton were lodged; next the two Englishmen hurriedly copying the inscription by the light of a flickering lantern; and, finally, the return trip with the heavy marble slab which had to be hauled up on to the roof of the mosque before daylight. In this secretive manner and by such stratagems were the first facts about the kingdom of Saba gathered, while the scholars back in Europe awaited confirmation of Cruttenden's sensational report that the site of Marib was providing the local tribesmen with gold coins, jewels, pearls, and marble statues, one of which, though with a smashed head in deference to Islamic law, the Englishman had seen in the Imam's garden. In view of these finds, it was now imperative that someone should actually reach Marib and verify these rumours of ruined palaces and temples described by the old Arab travellers, Hamdani, Masudi, and Idrisi. The first of these writers, in fact, refers to the columns of the Haram Bilqis, or Palace of Bilqis (the Arab name for the Queen of Sheba) as still standing, while elsewhere in the narratives of Arab travellers there is a reference to the throne of the queen perched on pillars over 100 feet high, a patent exaggeration. But it was obvious that much of ancient Marib still survived above ground, while priceless treasures were lying buried under the sands. To a considerable extent national prestige as well as scholarly interest was involved. Every European nation had explorers in the field all over the still unknown world. The French, for their part, had long had a good foothold in the Yemen, largely thanks to their doctors who had treated the imams and their families. And so it was that, in 1843, seven years after Cruttenden's visit to San'a and his report of the treasures to be found at Marib, the French Société Asiatique found a man both qualified and able to make the perilous journey into the interior of Arabia Felix.

He was Thomas Arnaud, a French pharmacist in the service of the Imam of San'a. Arnaud, despite his immense contribution to the history of Arabia, is an almost forgotten explorer and does not even rate an entry in the French dictionaries of biography; but fortunately he wrote an account of his journey. His report published in the April–May 1845 edition of the

Journal Asiatique tells the story of his travels. It is one of the great epics of exploration.

Thomas Joseph Arnaud de Lurs (Basses-Alpes) arrived at Marib in the year 1843 and was welcomed in a somewhat begrudging fashion by the local sheikhs who did, however, send a woman slave to give the traveller a full massage with fresh butter, a practical sign of hospitality in the desert. The rites of hospitality performed, his hosts proceeded to bombard him with questions – where had he come from, where was he going, and the key question: was he looking for buried treasure? The French pharmacist parried these continual and often dangerous questions with skill and wit, launching into a speech in which he asserted that his sole reason for travelling was to contemplate the marvels of the universe as created by Allah and, at the same time, to visit the places mentioned in the Holy Book, of which Marib with its great dam was one. As for buried treasure, he was not interested in such material things, as Providence had provided him with enough for his simple needs and all that he wanted was to copy the inscriptions on the walls of the Haram of Bilqis to prove to his friends that he had seen the places he described.

Yes, said the Arabs, that was all very well, but why didn't he pray in company with his fellow-travellers of the caravan? (Arnaud had to be careful about this query, since he had intimated that he was a Moslem but, at the same time, was determined not to betray his true faith – a predicament in which a number of explorers in those days found themselves.) Because, he replied, he had diarrhoea as a result of the fatigues of the journey and did not feel that he was in a pure enough state to bow in prayer. Many of his interrogators were not satisfied with this answer and continued to cross-examine him, whereupon Arnaud, perceiving his danger, lay down on the ground, covered himself with his robe, and pretended to go to sleep.

On 18 July 1843, the Frenchman reached Marib, 'a land where no other European had ever set foot; or if there was one before me, he never returned to tell the tale'.[1]

His reception in the village of Marib which is built on a *tall* beneath which lies the ancient capital of Sheba was at first cordial on account of an extraordinary tale told him by the inhabitants: namely, that ten or twelve years before a white man had arrived in Marib coming along the Incense Road from the Hadramaut (Oman) and had copied all the inscriptions he could find. Then, producing a letter which (they said) the genii must have delivered to him during the night, this mysterious visitor announced that his brother had just died and that he had therefore to return home; and the next night he departed without a guide or any escort. The people of Marib were certain that this person was a holy man who possessed the 'knowledge of the name' – that is, the ability to perform miracles. What is unusual about this story is that it was told all over the Yemen and can only refer to Carsten Niebuhr, the first European to penetrate this part of Arabia in 1761, although the German explorer had certainly never reached Marib. But his reputation had obviously become legendary with the passage of time, and his 'brother' in question was undoubtedly his companion, the botanist Dr Peter Forskäl, who had died on the road to San'a.

Arnaud, in the meantime, was at last able to visit the Haram Bilqis, or as we know it to-day, the Temple of Ilumquh, the moon-god worshipped by the Sabaeans. Here he was only given time to copy two inscriptions before he was hustled away. He had now become deeply suspect to the tribesmen who would no longer accept his excuses for not praying with them, and he began to be actually harassed in Marib itself

1. Thomas Arnaud, 'Relation d'un voyage à Mareb (Saba) dans l'Arabie meridionale, enterpris en 1843', *Journal Asiatique*, ser. iv, vol v (April–May, 1845) p 325.

where he tried to record the beautifully inscribed stones which were, and still are, used as lintels for doors or were built into the walls of the houses. In fact, the whole town was practically entirely built from the ruins of the ancient city, as the sculpted and inscribed slabs of marble proved. Seeing him examining their houses and then stopping to copy an inscription, the women hung out of their windows, screaming, 'Clear off, sorcerer! infidel! Don't try to bring troubles upon our country!' and they shouted with derision at the Frenchman who calls them *'ces furies sabéennes'*.

But even though Arnaud was continuously tormented and frequently on the point of being actually murdered, he survived his journey to Marib and has the very great distinction of being the first European to see the two great towers of the mighty dam. Even here he was harassed, for when he began to copy the inscriptions which proclaimed the names of the kings who had undertaken the repairs, he found himself threatened by a loaded rifle and prevented from surveying the huge construction further. To add to his troubles, he was now struck down by sunstroke which his Arab companions found very amusing. Even so, he brought back his plans and inscriptions safely, though at the expense of losing his sight for ten months following his amazing journey. He concludes his report with these words: 'I spent nearly ten months in a dreadful state of blindness, but at the moment, thanks to God, my sight is beginning to be restored.'[1]

Arnaud's epic journey had a curious sequel. It appears that while he was convalescing at the house of the French orientalist Fulgence Fresnel he made a model of the Marib dam in wet sand, from which his host drew a plan sent post-haste to the editors of the *Journal Asiatique* in Paris. One of these editors, Grangeret de Lagrange, lost the Fresnel drawings of the dam

1. *op cit*, p 345.

and of the ruins of Marib in the street; and though a large sum of money was offered for their recovery, the drawings were never found. At the same time, it was known that Arnaud himself had drawn maps of the Marib area despite the fact that he was not a surveyor and had been followed everywhere by hostile Arabs pointing rifles at him. But these original drawings were thought to have been destroyed during the siege of Paris in 1871, when many of the libraries of learned societies were deliberately burnt or looted by the mob. Happily, thirty years after the explorer had made his drawings *in situ* at Marib, some unknown person returned them to the Société Asiatique which published them in the 1874 edition of its *Journal*. These plans of Arnaud, despite the dangers and difficulties the explorer faced in obtaining them, are so accurate that the visitor to Marib to-day can quickly and easily get his bearings by referring to them.

The observer can readily see for himself how the whole province which was once famous for its gardens and orchards is now a desert, supporting scarcely any plant life apart from the tamarisk trees along the beds of the ancient canals.

The second traveller to reach the capital of Saba was a Jew born in Turkey and naturalized in France, Joseph Halévy, who arrived at Marib in 1870, just twenty-seven years after Thomas Arnaud. Arnaud the pharmacist was, of course, an amateur Arabist, whereas Halévy was a professional orientalist, already familiar with the Himyarite language and the history of the kingdom of Saba. Because of his erudition, he had been commissioned by the French Académie des Inscriptions et Belles-Lettres to undertake a mission to the Yemen in order to search out and copy all the Sabaean and Himyarite inscriptions he could locate in his travels. He proposed to journey through the Yemen in the guise of a rabbi, for there were certain advantages in so doing. In the first place, as a rabbi he would have no need to dissemble about his religion, as Thomas Arnaud, a devout Catholic, had had to dissemble about his. In the second, there were at this time some 60,000 Jews living in towns and villages throughout the Yemen, and while they were openly despised by the Moslems, they were not officially persecuted. This relative tolerance was due to the fact that Jews had been settled in the area centuries before the rise of Islam and they were often the only group in the community who, as well as being literate, were also skilled artisans, jewellery being their speciality. Even so, their condition was wretched by any civilized standards, for not only did the Moslems claim to have power of life and death over them and the right to confiscate their property with impunity, but they could continually harass them by such petty regulations as forbidding them to wear white, red, or green clothing and to ride any animal but a donkey, from which they had to dismount on the approach of a Moslem.

Joseph Halévy as a member of the Alliance Israëlite Universelle knew all about conditions for his co-religionists in the Yemen, and he must have known that he ventured into that country at the peril of his life, for it was about this period, the 1870s, that the Yemenite Jews had already begun to flee to Jerusalem where they believed 'the great Rothschild' would give them a grant of land. But even more vexatious than threats were the real indignities inflicted upon him as a Jew. He writes:

My guide, even though I had paid him for the complete journey, abandoned me in the mountains. Tormented by thirst in the midst of this terrible desert, confused by dunes of moving sand, I was lucky to reach a camp of nomads who existed almost exclusively on a diet of camel milk . . . My next guide, a Hercules of a man, not only robbed me of everything I had, but threatened to kill me . . . And when I joined a caravan coming from the Hadramaut, the camel-men took great pleasure in inflicting on me every indignity they could think of.[1]

But despite the dangers and discomforts of his incredible journey, Halévy saw so many new and wonderful things that he pressed on regardless of his sufferings. He discovered a number of Sabaean and Minaean cities which had been completely lost for some 2,000 years and which, incidentally, have been lost again since the Yemen was closed to outsiders during the reigns of the fanatical and bloodthirsty imams of our own century. We can take as typical of these imams and their rule,[2] Imam Yahya ibn Muhamad (1904–1948). Yahya himself was assassinated in 1948. The eldest of his fourteen legitimate sons, the Crown Prince Ahmed, though the most hated man in the country, managed to die in bed, in 1962. The second son, Muhammad, was drowned, 1933. The third, Hasan, was killed, 1962, fighting in the civil war. The fourth and fifth sons were drunkards and jailed for riotous living by their father Yahya. When offered their liberty, they declined, stating that they preferred to stay in prison as it gave them more freedom than the palace. And of the other nine sons, one was beheaded in 1955; another died in prison of 'heart failure', 1948; another was shot by a firing-squad, 1962; and two others were beheaded, one in 1948, the other in 1955. The dynasty ended with the abdication and flight of Imam Ahmed who had worked assiduously during his fourteen-year reign to liquidate all those of his family whom he regarded as rivals, in particular, of course, his brothers.

1. J. Halévy, 'Rapport sur une mission archéologique dans le Yemen', *Journal Asiatique* ser. vi, vol xix (1872) p 67.
2. The title *imam* is properly applied to the leader of prayers in a mosque. An imam is not, however, a priest for Islam has no priesthood. As applied to the rulers of the Yemen, the title is equivalent to Khalifa (Caliph).

During the entire period of Yahya and Ahmed's rule from around 1904 to 1962, no European archaeologist had been allowed near the magnificent Sabaean ruins, most of which were now buried under the sand, while the larger monuments, including Marib itself, had been partially or wholly destroyed by Egyptian bombs during the civil war of the sixties between the so-called royalists and the republicans.

Joseph Halévy was at least beyond the reach of the Imam once he had left San'a and so was able with immense labour and real heroism to set about collecting Himyarite inscriptions along the old Incense Road from Sirwah to Nadjran, though he was *never* allowed to pursue his harmless work of copying these records in peace. During the midday halt not far from Marib, for instance, he saw a mound from which projected the columns and steles so characteristic of the buried cities of ancient Sheba; and making an excuse to his guide, he ran over to these ruins which were encircled within a high wall and found within a mass of fallen masonry, some of it covered with inscriptions. But was he allowed to copy them? Certainly not. His guide now appeared on the scene, haranguing him for absenting himself in order to look for buried treasure. All the explorer could do under the circumstances was to report the name of this place. It was Kharibet-Se'oud, not seen again by a Western traveller until H. St John Philby, who calls the site Khirbat Sa'ud, visited it in 1936. Philby describes the very attractive temple which lay in ruins, apparently shaken down by an earthquake, and remarks on the number of inscriptions some of which he was able to copy down, where poor Halévy was denied this opportunity.

The walls are massive and well built [Philby writes]. The interior is full of ruined masonry and sand-covered mounds . . . One nice bit of stone with an inscription was in use as a headstone of a modern grave. My guides kindly removed it under cover of darkness, and it is now in the British Museum.[1]

One can imagine what would have happened to the Jew Joseph Halévy if he had helped himself to a Moslem gravestone: he would have been murdered on the spot. As it was, he was in great danger when he came to Sirwah, the second of the great cities of Saba, notable for its huge elliptical temple dedicated to the moon-god Ilumquh. In the centre of this temple stood a stone prism seventy feet long, three feet high, and one and a half feet thick covered with the most famous of all Himyarite inscriptions, over 1,000 words in length. Halévy was, of course, longing to copy this magnificent record which, he perceived with some apprehension, was being used by the local inhabitants for carding wool and washing clothes. Seeing the stranger copying the inscription, the men shouted that he was a sorcerer, whereupon the women began howling like banshees, and everyone rushed at him with sticks, stones, and rifles, threatening to kill him. Keeping his nerve, he announced that he was a citizen of the holy city of Jerusalem and that his death at their hands would inevitably bring misery upon them, their children, and their flocks and herds. At this they ceased to threaten him and retired to the door of the building for a conference. The Frenchman took this opportunity of copying six more lines of the inscription, but they confiscated his paper and sent him away. He decided that he had better get as far away from Sirwah as he could, and fleeing this wonderful but dangerous Sabaean city, he spent the night sleeping in a cave, quite alone in the middle of a hostile country. However, Halévy was at least fortunate in that he could rely on finding a Jewish community in almost every sizeable town and village he passed through, showing that the Jews who had settled all

1. Philby, *op cit*, p 126.

over the Arabian peninsula no doubt as far back as the time of King Solomon were still able to survive in this fanatical land. They have, of course, all emigrated to Israel within the last fifty years and the towns where they lived and worked as goldsmiths and silversmiths are now devoid of skilled jewellers. Their ornaments which were about the only works of art produced in the Yemen have now completely disappeared from the bazaars where the Jewish craftsmen had their little shops alongside the sellers of the Yemenite dagger, the universally-worn *jambiya*, and it is really rather a waste of the tourist's time to search for these pretty objects in the alleys of the souks. He or she must wait for reproductions to arrive from the backroom workshops of Cairo and Alexandria.

Joseph Halévy's epic journey, together with the explorations of Thomas Arnaud, had literally recreated the old kingdom of Saba to the extent that it was now possible for scholars, comfortably working in their libraries, to write the history of a region that had been totally lost for almost 2,000 years. There was no difficulty in translating the hundreds of inscriptions which the two travellers had brought back to Europe at the risk of their lives. The Himyarite language and script are easy to read for philologists expert in the old Semitic tongues. One such specialist was the Austrian scholar Eduard Glaser who was to complete the work begun by the two Frenchmen, journeying throughout the Yemen for fourteen years between 1882 and 1894. Glaser brought out of South Arabia a collection of 264 rare manuscripts, 1,032 Himyarite and Sabaean inscriptions (one of which was 130 lines long) and the first accurate maps of the Yemen. For the first time, we find a European travelling in comparative freedom and safety in this country of feuding tribes; and this was made possible because the fortunate explorer was no longer obliged to travel like his two predecessors – on foot and donkey-back, half-begging his way from tribe to tribe and continually harassed because of his religion. Glaser was liberally financed by German learned societies, officially sponsored by the Austrian government, and placed under the protection, uncertain though this was, of the Turks who by 1871 had occupied the Yemen and garrisoned the principal towns and villages. Moreover, German-speaking merchants, engineers, and doctors were now the privileged visitors to a land which had been for centuries the domain both the English and the French had hoped, though without success, to add to their sphere of influence.

Eduard Glaser, then, could be said to have finished the work which Carsten Niebuhr had begun 200 years before. Certainly not much more epigraphical material was needed to complete the official records of the South Arabian kingdoms. It was now up to the archaeologists to give a deeper meaning to the inscriptions of Sabaean monarchs extolling their achievements in the usual bombastic language of oriental potentates. But it soon became obvious to the universities prepared to sponsor a properly organized dig at Marib or any of the other Himyarite cities that conditions in the Yemen were again inauspicious. The response of the Yemeni authorities to inquiries from British, French, and German archaeologists was invariably negative, the official excuse for refusing permits to excavate being, once again, 'the unsettled state of the tribes'. One must admit that this was partially true; what with the endless political intrigues, the border disputes, and the blood-feuds. But underlying the refusal to grant the necessary permission was the old feudal suspicion of the outsider poking his nose into local affairs. In other words, it was one thing to permit a lone infidel to copy down the magic symbols of the ancient genii as Arnaud and Halévy had done, though this was suspicious enough; it was altogether different when these foreigners wanted to come in battalions with the intention of digging up the treasures belonging by right to the local tribe. For such was the attitude of the Yemeni, whether prince or peasant, towards the archaeologist.

The American Wendell Phillips came nearest to realizing the ambition of every archaeologist to excavate as rich and undisturbed a site as Marib. With this prize in mind, Dr Phillips had first instituted the American Foundation for the Study of Man and then organized a full-scale expedition of some thirty specialists supported by enough equipment to transport and set up a camp with all the comforts of an American hotel. With a team of archaeologists, Arabists, epigraphists, field directors, business managers, interpreters, motor transport specialists, administrative assistants, geologists, physicians, surveyors, draftsmen, photographers, and native servants, the Phillips expedition made its first dig at Hajar Kohlan in Beihan, south-west Arabia, and unearthed the capital of the ancient kingdom of Qataban, a city called Timna. It was a splendid beginning for the expedition which had triumphed over all the multifarious local difficulties, like the demand of the Sultan of Mukalla that Phillips should give him a steam-roller if the Americans wanted to get customs clearance for his equipment. But Beihan was a tribal area of the British-administered Western Aden protectorate and even sultans were aware in those days that they could not with impunity provoke the British lion; but it was a very different kettle of fish in the independent state to the north. North Yemen was a feudal society, and while it had a sort of central government, almost every minister was a brother or son of the King, Imam Ahmed. In fact, it was one of the brothers, His Royal Highness Prince Abdullah, minister of foreign affairs, who invited Wendell Phillips to come to his country to discuss Marib, though no one seems to have known why. Phillips, of course, was overjoyed and arrived for his audience well supplied with gifts: he was learning after the steam-roller lesson at Mukalla how affairs are conducted in this part of the world. And so when he presented himself to the King, he first apologized for the paucity of his offerings and then ceremonially presented to His Majesty a pair of binoculars, a rifle, a pistol, ammunition, an electric fan, a wireless, a typewriter, a Polaroid camera, and case after case of Coca-Cola, canned food, and bathroom requisites. The king examined this assortment of articles and remarked 'The Prophet Muhammad accepted even small gifts; for it is the spirit behind the gift, not the gift itself, that matters.' Phillips thereupon received the royal warrant to excavate at Marib. It was an historic date in the annals of archaeology.[1]

Unfortunately for Phillips, the local chieftains at Marib cared no more for King Ahmed in his palace at Taiz 300 miles away across the mountains than they did for President Truman in the White House at Washington 5,000 miles away across the ocean. For when the archaeologists announced to the governor of Marib that they were about to remove the sand from the Haram Bilqis (Temple of Ilumquh), the governor asked, 'Do you have permission to excavate?' This seemingly artless question sums up perfectly the attitude of a Yemeni tribesman to foreign archaeologists and distant potentates. So in its way does the attitude of King Ahmed who, when called to for help, ignored the whole affair and never replied to a single cable. Perhaps that was even harder for the Americans to understand than the curious behaviour of the local authorities who found reasons for delaying work so outrageous that the archaeologists were at their wits' end. The locals, of course, were playing a game whose rules no outsider could ever hope to understand, since the rules were expressly designed to baffle him. Thus, one day the local governor refused to advance any

1. The story of the expedition is told in Wendell Phillips's *Qataban and Sheba*, London: Gollancz, 1955.

of the expedition's funds over which he had been given control as part of the deal with the King. The next he demanded that the workers be driven back from the site where digging had begun three miles across the sand to the mosque at Marib for midday prayers. This meant, in effect, that the whole of the afternoons would be lost. On other occasions, he complained that the workmen were not paid enough or did not have enough water or were needed for work in the village and so on. But his most clever stratagem for thwarting the treasure-seeking foreigners was the ruse of the store-room key. The store-room was a room in the fort at Marib, a locked room containing at least 600 alabaster statues, most of them inscribed in the Himyarite language. They represented a priceless archaeological treasure which happened to have been saved because the local people who had found the artefacts while quarrying for building material suspected that one day they might fetch a small sum in the San'a bazaar. But when Dr Albert Jamme, the Belgian epigraphist, asked if he could take latex squeezes of the inscriptions carved on the statues, he was told the key of the store-room was not available for the moment, but that it would be forthcoming 'tomorrow'. On the morrow the doctor was told the key had now been traced to San'a. Several days later, the governor announced that the key had been found and that it was on its way 'in a small plane, as it was only a small key'. A week later, with no sign of plane or key, the news was that it was coming by a courier but this man alas! had fallen sick on the way. And so the farce continued, with more cables to the King which were, of course, never answered.[1]

One cannot help thinking that many of the expedition's problems would have been solved by the dispensing of more and bigger largesses in the right quarters. On the other hand, there is no doubt that tribal feuding together with the jockey-

1. *op cit*, pp 234–5.

ing for power between the King and his brothers – one of whom was the virtual ruler of eastern Yemen and hence of Marib – was incomprehensible to the American professors who found themselves harassed by petty officials, eventually with disastrous results. The climax of their troubles came at the worst possible time when after weeks of work they had managed to dig out from the sand and to erect the six great pillars of the Temple of Ilumquh which formed the imposing peristyle of the semi-circular shrine to the moon-god. It quickly became obvious to the archaeologists that these columns, temporarily propped up by stones and timbers, needed cement foundations to hold them in place, but there was no way of bringing in the cement. Suddenly one of the pillars swayed and then toppled, falling against its neighbour and so bringing down the entire row like dominoes. During the collapse, a Yemeni workman was injured and one of the columns shattered. This was the end of the project. The expedition photographer was arrested; the Belgian epigraphist was refused permission to make further latex copies of the inscriptions; and soldiers were posted inside the expedition headquarters. All further work was subjected to constant and deliberate interference. Finally, despite requests to the King for an audience, cables to Washington, appeals to the President of the United States, the Secretary General of the United Nations, and the directors of various learned societies, Wendell Phillips realized that his position was becoming untenable and that the personal safety of his team was endangered. Like a small army completely cut off, the only course of action left was to flee, without waiting for permission to stay or to leave. One morning the nineteen members of the expedition put their carefully worked-out plan of escape into execution: they boarded their Power Wagons with what they could save of their personal belongings and roared off from their camp, pursued by a *goum* of the Yemeni camel corps. The Power

Wagons, of course, won the race; the archaeologists got safely across the border into the Aden Protectorate; and the ruins of Marib were left to sink back into the sand. It is the abandoned excavations of the 1953 American expedition that the visitor to the capital of the kingdom of Sheba sees to-day.

Ruins of temples and, of course, the seemingly indestructible towers of the great dam. And to the social historian, this mighty construction is far more evocative than the famous ovoid temples to the sun, moon, and star gods. The Marib dam encapsulates, as it were, the quintessence of the Sabaean social and economic life, for a work of such magnitude implies tremendous knowledge, skill, and national unity, all harnessed for the benefit of every citizen of the kingdom. The idea of controlling running water by a dam is, of course, one of the most ancient of agricultural concepts, and it is easy to build a mud embankment for the irrigation of fields bordering a stream. But somewhere around the ninth century BC, the kings of Marib undertook to dam a wadi nearly half a mile wide and to irrigate tens of thousands of acres of desert. The project called for a twenty-five-foot high embankment across the wadi Dhana, with massive retaining towers at either end of the dam, sluices, sediment basins, and canals the like of which are found nowhere else in the ancient world. This complex and sophisticated system was made possible by the erection of the two stone towers some fifty feet high designed to control the flood waters by means of sluice gates which could be raised or lowered to release the stored water into the main canals which fanned out into twenty-two branches, each with its retaining walls. Eduard Glaser who explored the dam in 1886 reported that much of the earthen embankment was still in place in his day, though the central section had been washed away in the great flood of the sixth century AD which destroyed not only the dam but spelt the end of Saba itself. Glaser was able to survey the system and made the best sketches that we have even to-day. He states that the wall of the dam was some twenty-five feet high, shaped like an isosceles triangle, and faced on its upstream side with small sharp stones so strongly mortared into position that it was impossible to dislodge them.

This astonishing undertaking, which still survives in a ruinous condition and which, incidentally, still awaits detailed study, was begun about 875 BC and religiously maintained for almost 1,500 years, the accepted date of the destruction of the dam wall being *circa* AD 600. One says 'religiously' advisedly, since the kings who ordered the construction and who were responsible for its repairs were, like the rulers of all Semitic tribes, also priests. As priest-kings, they were guardians of the people's welfare and mindful of their sacred duty. Their inscriptions recording the nature and extent of the reparations date from around 500 BC and continue through the centuries up to the reign of King Sharahbil Ya'fur who in AD 450 requisitioned 20,000 labourers from the nearby kingdoms of Himyar and Hadramaut to assist his national workforce with the necessary repairs. There is one last inscription put up by the Abyssinian viceroy after the conquest of Saba. The stela announces that the rations supplied to the workers included:

   200,000 sheep and goats
    50,000 sacks of flour
    26,000 packages of dates

with 3,000 camels and oxen designated for transport and haulage.

The visitor to the Marib dam can still see that inscription lying in the rubble beneath the shadow of the great tower of the northern abutment.

To-day, the town of Marib, perched atop the palaces of the

Sabaean capital, houses a few hundred poor tribesmen, and it gives the impression of being as remote and inhospitable as when Thomas Arnaud arrived here a century and a half ago. From the rubble and the sand dunes still emerge the monoliths of the Sabaean palaces and nearby rise up the ruined columns of the great temples to the moon-god. Out in the empty wadi stand the towers of the mightiest dam ever built in the ancient world, but not a drop of water is now caught by its sluice gates or channelled into the fields and orchards which gave the name of 'Happy' to Arabia. Rather, the best description of Marib is still that of Muhammad who may well have stopped there with a caravan en route to the incense groves of Oman:

> For the people of Saba there was a sign in their homeland: two gardens, one on the right hand and the other on the left. Allah commanded them: Eat of that which your Lord has provided for you and be grateful. You have a pleasant land and a Lord most forgiving. Yet they turned away from the truth. So we afflicted them with a devastating flood and converted their two excellent gardens into gardens bearing bitter fruits, tamarisks, and a few thorn trees . . .[1]

That is exactly what the visitor sees to-day – tamarisks and thorn trees which grow along the banks of the old canals and lying about in the sand the broken pillars and inscribed memorials of a nation which even the Roman legions were unable to conquer.

1. *The Quran*, translated by Muhammad Zafrulla Khan, London: Curzon Press, 1971, Chapter 34, 11. 16–22, p 422.

Terracotta figurines of people and animals engaged in everyday
occupations remind us that the vanished world of 3000 BC was
not all that different from our own

Mohenjo-Daro, one of the Indus Valley settlements that made up
a massive and advanced Bronze Age culture

Dr Oudney's important discovery of this Roman mausoleum in 1822 authoritatively linked the Saharan oasis of Germa with Garama, southernmost boundary of the Roman Empire

Crumbling mud-brick pyramids mark the burial ground of kings of the Garamantes – a populous and prosperous nation which once controlled the most important caravan route across the Sahara

Part 2
Asia – the Orient

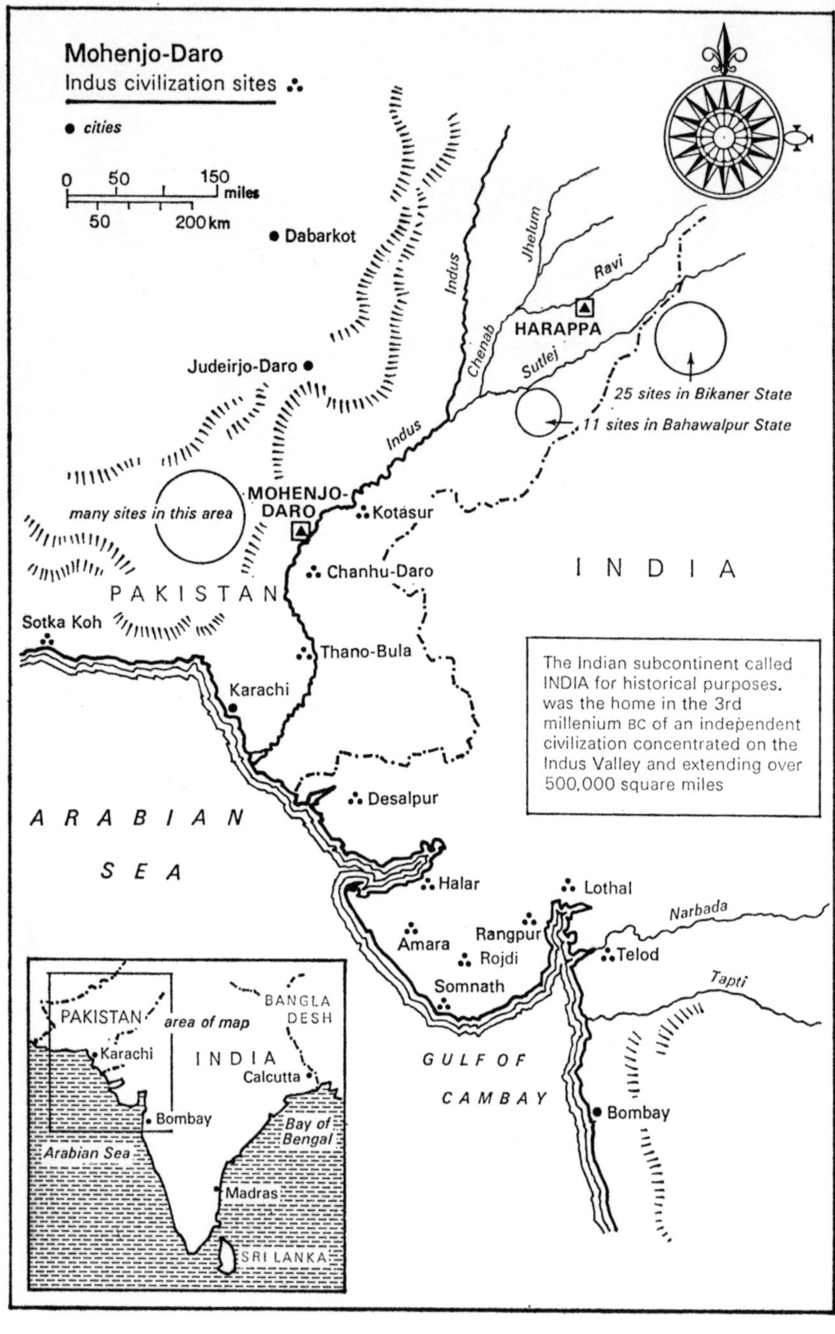

Mohenjo-Daro
Indus civilization sites
cities
0 50 150 miles
50 200 km
Dabarkot
Judeirjo-Daro
Indus
Chenab
Jhelum
Ravi
Sutlej
HARAPPA
25 sites in Bikaner State
11 sites in Bahawalpur State
MOHENJO-DARO
Kotasur
Chanhu-Daro
INDIA
PAKISTAN
many sites in this area
Sotka Koh
Thano-Bula
Karachi
The Indian subcontinent called INDIA for historical purposes. was the home in the 3rd millenium BC of an independent civilization concentrated on the Indus Valley and extending over 500,000 square miles
Desalpur
A R A B I A N
S E A
Halar
Lothal
Narbada
Amara
Rangpur
Rojdi
Telod
Somnath
Tapti
GULF OF
CAMBAY
Bombay
PAKISTAN
area of map
BANGLA DESH
Karachi
INDIA
Calcutta
Bombay
Bay of Bengal
Arabian Sea
Madras
SRI LANKA

Mohenjo-Daro

The story of Mohenjo-Daro begins soon after 3000 BC when a race of people of whom we know nothing built a number of cities, towns, and villages in that region of the Indian sub-continent called the Punjab, or Land of the Five Rivers. For want of a more specific term, we refer to this strange and at present unexplained historical phenomenon as the Indus Valley civilization. We are only gradually finding out that this people's homeland was greater in extent than that of any other Bronze Age society and that their civilization was just as advanced as that of Egypt and Sumer. Yet by 1750 BC their settlements, including large cities like Mohenjo-Daro and Harappa, had not only ceased to exist, but had vanished so completely that there is no mention of them in even the oldest of the records that have come down to us. Darius, the Persian king of kings, for instance, who conquered the Indus Valley in 522 BC, met no resistance from, and knew nothing about, the once-powerful nation whose territory he occupied. Nor did Alexander the Great who marched through the Land of Five Rivers 200 years later without any idea at all that the vast mounds of rubble beside the river banks were the ruins of walled cities which would undoubtedly have held up his army far longer than King Porus's elephants. The same total ignorance of this, the most extensive civilization of the pre-classical world, was typical of all those conquerors and occupants of the region, from the Greek dynasts of the seven-teen colonies planted in the Indus Valley to the Buddhists,

Brahmins, Moslems, and British who came and departed in their turn. None of them, in brief, ever saw a vestige of the seventy or more centres of population which constituted one of the largest of the ancient oriental cultures.

Historically, then, Mohenjo-Daro exists, as it were, in a vacuum, which is why a visitor to the excavations requires to exert a considerable effort of imagination in order to people the immense ruins with beings he can identify with. To begin with, this Bronze Age city has none of the spectacular beauty of the Greek and Roman cities, with their marble columns, triumphal arches, theatres, baths, and fountains – all familiar fixtures of the urban scene to-day. The layman expecting to see these pleasant relics, like the photographer looking for picture-postcard views, will be disappointed. In truth, Mohenjo-Daro is so old, so vast, and so ponderous with its masses of dried brick that it is difficult to believe that it was ever a living city at all. The attention can easily wander, and it is no use the professional archaeologist scolding us because we are not excited by, say, the architectonic subtleties of the timber-bonding. The fact is that we are likely to learn more about Mohenjo-Daro by gazing at the bronze figurine of a dancing girl unearthed during the excavations and now on display in the national museum than by studying the construction of the podium of the State Granary.

So let us be unorthodox and start our visit by examining the statuette of that girl with the bunched curls, large eyes, flat nose, and rows of bracelets on her arms (the right hand resting provocatively on her hip). Here is the evidence we needed that these wall-less houses at Mohenjo-Daro were once in-habited and these empty streets once trod by real people; for we have seen this girl in exactly this pose in many places all over the Near and Middle East. Her stance as she rests, hand on hip, after dancing to an all-male audience is familiar, and the number of bracelets on her arms is the traditional proof of success among girls of her profession, to-day as 5,000 years ago. So the little bronze is proof that the old ruins were not only inhabited by the usual categories of citizens – priests, merchants, craftsmen and soldiers – all going about their business in the dry as dust manner described in the textbooks, but that these citizens, when the day's work was done, had the same ideas about entertainment, for instance, as we have to-day and as Richard Burton who visited these parts a century ago found were in vogue even then.

> Mahtab, the Moonbeam, floats forward so lightly that trace of exertion is imperceptible: softly and slowly waving her white arms and pink palms, she unexpectedly stands close to you, then, turning with a pirouette she sinks back, retires, and stands motionless as wax-work . . .[1]

Other figurines and statues from the Indus Valley, some in stone like that of a heavy-eyed, bearded man with a long nose and thick lips, others in terracotta of women engaged in household occupations, and others again of bulls, elephants, rhinoceroses, pigs, monkeys, and dogs remind us that the world of the third millennium BC was not all that different from our own and yet emphasize the mystery of this extraordinary ruin. For what happened to Mohenjo-Daro, Chanhu-Daro, Harappa, Amri, Kot Diji, and the scores of other towns and villages so far unearthed in the Indus Valley? Why were their very names, as well as their locations, forgotten within a few years of their decline and fall? The question is all the more significant in that some of these cities were manifestly the capitals of a highly advanced political, social, and economic complex comparable with the kingdoms of Mesopotamia. Yet the reason for Mohenjo-Daro's complete disappearance from

---

1. Richard Burton, *Sind Revisited*, London: Bentley, 1877, vol ii, p 207.

the annals of mankind has not been answered. Let us try and
see why.

To begin with, none of the written records, even the earliest of
them, makes any mention whatsoever of an Indian civilization
contemporaneous with the civilizations of Mesopotamia and
Egypt. There is, for instance, no reference in the extensive
Sumerian or Akkadian documents to those far-off cities with
whom Ur, Lagash, and Babylon must have had commercial
relations, unless a land called Dilmun (meaning 'where the
sun rises') actually refers to the Indus Valley. But it is certain
that the vast trade which was eventually to build up first
between the Far Orient and Asia Minor and then between the
Far East and the Mediterranean would have already begun in
the third millennium BC. There are numerous, albeit obscure,
references in the Sumerian records to distant places which
supplied the Mesopotamian cities with gold, silver, copper,
lapis lazuli, beads, certain kinds of wood, pearls, and ivory.
Mention of the last of these imports is the evidence historians
are looking for to support the theory that international trade
between the Indus Valley city-states and those of Mesopotamia
was a fact. For ivory and ivory-working are, and always have
been, essentially Indian. Five thousand years ago elephants
must have been plentiful in the forests of north-west India and
no doubt their tusks were brought to the big cities of Mohenjo-
Daro and Harappa as the centres of the ivory trade. From
here they were shipped to the West across the Arabian Sea.
The ordinary citizens of Ur, of course, knew nothing about
Mohenjo-Daro, not even where it was situated, or what its
people were like. Whether their merchants, in particular the
import-export traders, were better informed we have no way
of knowing, but the commercial documents continually refer
to the lands called Dilmun, Makkan, and Meluhha from

whence came the cargoes of exotic woods and much-prized ivory.

Unfortunately, the classical historians are also silent on the subject of the Indus Valley civilization, which is not mentioned by even the historians of Alexander who in 326 BC accompanied the King on his march from Samarkand down the Indus river to the Arabian Sea and were, therefore, literally within sight of the ancient Indian cities. These military historians, who were, in effect, the predecessors of the nineteenth-century war correspondents, evidently saw nothing of Mohenjo-Daro or any other of the Valley settlements, for they would certainly have reported on them if they had, as they had reported on the wonders of Babylon and Persepolis. But the fact is that once his army had crossed the Hindu Kush, neither Alexander himself nor his companions quite knew where they were, or whither they were going. Without maps or compasses, they marched onwards, as though driven by the fanatical ambition of a young man who had been told that his destiny was to conquer the world. It is no wonder that the Greeks actually thought when they first saw the river Indus that they had reached the Nile.

Actually, Mohenjo-Daro, Harappa, and all the centres of the Indus Valley so far identified have only appeared on the screen of history by an accident. For the discovery of a city which was not only lost in the geographical sense but had never existed at all in historical records was made neither by an explorer nor an archaeologist, but by a very matter-of-fact British engineer.

In 1857, John Brunton arrived in Karachi with a party of twenty engineers whose commission was to build a railway up the Indus river valley. Brunton was characteristic of his country and his time, a typical Victorian who travelled in many parts of the world building the roads and railways which linked the farthest outposts of the Empire to the mother country. He lived to be eighty-six years and worked continually from the age of fifteen to seventy-eight, when he finally retired. He built a hospital in the Crimea for Florence Nightingale, the Sind Railway, the Milan tramway system, and an ice and soda-water works at Kotru on the Indus river. He was the type of man who, when attacked by a rabid wolf, 'having nothing to defend myself with, waved my big sun-topi and made loud demonstrations'.[1] He always looked after his men and saw to it that they had good clean drinking water long before the connection between typhoid, amoebic dysentery, and polluted water had been discovered. And his attitude towards the world was that of a simple English gentleman: he comments upon the Indian custom of cutting off the nose and ears of suspected malefactors, exclaiming, 'Fancy such in-justice and cruelty!' At the same time, he was always interested in local idiosyncrasies and gives us a splendid description of Pir Mango near Karachi, the small oasis famous for its holy alligators, or Muggurs, as they were called. According to Brunton, these animals lined up at the water's edge once a day when the priest shouted '*Ow, Ow*' (meaning 'Come, come'). They were then fed pieces of goat which was slaughtered daily for their benefit. The 'King of the Muggurs', who lived by himself and was painted vermilion, received the head and horns which he smashed with one crunch. Brunton deprecates the habit of what he terms 'larky young officers' throwing soda-water bottles tied together into the jaws of the sacred reptiles, and no doubt the alligators, after swallowing the bottles, would have deprecated it even more.[2]

Before leaving Karachi to survey the route of the Indus

1. *John Brunton's Book*, Cambridge: University Press, 1939, p 94.
2. *op cit*, pp 108–9.

Railway, the engineer tells us that he had heard of a ruined city called Brahminabad in the Great Desert of the Sind and he anticipated that this old site would provide him with what he calls 'balast' for his railway track, especially since he understood that the city had been built of kiln-fired brick. Nobody knew where exactly Brahminabad lay, but the engineer was determined to find it and so set out across the desert with his camels and a supply of forage and provisions. On the way he met an 'intelligent native' who knew the location of the ruin and after two days' march they arrived at the site of what was to become Pakistan's most famous historical monument, Mohenjo-Daro, the capital of one of the world's first civilizations.

Fortunately for history, Brunton was an intelligent and observant traveller, and it was he who gave us the first description of this lost city. He writes that it was situated on the banks of a dried-up river and consisted of three sections, the largest of which was surrounded by a wall twenty feet thick and fourteen feet high. He suggests that this area (which we know to-day as the Citadel) represented the manufacturing or commercial portion of the city, while a large ruin on the east bank of the old river bed was 'the Royal palace which I concluded to be the residence of courtiers and the nobility of ancient days'. From the size of the place and the height of what was still standing above ground, he concluded that his lost city must have been of great importance commercially.

Brunton made as careful an examination of the ruins as he could in the time available and undertook some rough and ready excavations, finding a hoard of coins in an earthenware pot, some 'debris of a lapidary' (by which he apparently meant some engraved stones), and some steatite seals, these last of paramount interest to scholars since they suggested that the unknown people who built this lost city had evolved a script. As for the British engineer, his quick survey of the ruined city completed, he returned to his base camp and organized the transference of the kiln-fired bricks to the embankment of the new railway. So while John Brunton could be said to have partially discovered Mohenjo-Daro, he could also be charged with having partially destroyed it.

But in any case, his discovery was forgotten, and he with it. The credit for locating the lost city is now given to an Indian member of British-India's archaeological department, R. D. Banerji, who is reported in most textbooks as the 'discoverer in 1922 of the great mounds at Mohenjo-Daro'.

But neither John Brunton's factual report of his findings at Brahminabad nor R. D. Banerji's rediscovery of the same site some seventy-five years later brought the Indus Valley civilization any nearer, for several decades were to pass before any archaeologist, amateur or professional, even visited the site. Mohenjo-Daro was still historically non-existent: there is not even a mention of it in the 1935 edition of the *Cambridge History of India* and only a passing reference to 'seals of unknown date and origin which are said to have been found from time to time among the remains of brick structures at Harappa'.[1] It was, however, the superb carving and beautiful lettering of these seals which finally prompted the archaeologists of British India to investigate the ruins of the lost cities of the Indus Valley. The task was enormous in view of the area to be covered – estimated to be nearly half a million square miles – the lack of trained field workers, and the usual shortage of funds. Moreover, this part of India was littered with mounds and monuments. Where, then, to begin? During the last days of the *raj*, Sir John Marshall, the Director-General of Archaeology in India, decided to start work at Mohenjo-Daro in the

1. *Cambridge History of India*, Cambridge: University Press, 1935, p 618.

winter of 1923–24, since he knew from John Brunton's report that this huge mound was yielding quantities of burnt brick and, more significant, specimens of steatite seals with their mysterious writings. So two Indian assistants and later Sir John himself undertook extensive operations which have continued, with interruptions during times of war, civil strife, and natural calamities, from the twenties up to the present. During the last fifty years, in fact, so many other sites belonging to the Indus Valley civilizations have been identified that there are not enough archaeologists to excavate them, while the physical difficulties alone make it impossible now ever to reach the lowest levels of the river settlements. The early excavators at Mohenjo-Daro, for instance, had no sooner sunk a shaft than the sides began to collapse; and worse, as soon as fresh masonry was uncovered, it began rapidly to crumble away. The whole site, in fact, had become so impregnated with salt that a shower of rain produced a mass of crystals which destroyed the newly-exposed walls.

But despite the difficulties encountered by the archaeologists, visitors to Mohenjo-Daro can see at least the general lay-out of the great city, walk along its original streets, or wander in and out of the houses in which the citizens lived. The excavations have been rather hastily done and are, in any case, still incomplete. In fact, total excavation will never be possible, for the primordial Mohenjo-Daro now lies below the water-level of the plain. Deep diggings which were undertaken in the 1950s when enthusiasm for the new and exciting site was highest had to be abandoned some twenty-five feet down: the excavators were unable to control a multitude of small rivulets which caused their trenches and cuttings to collapse. This setback was disappointing because without reaching the foundations of the city, the mystery of its origin could not be solved, the mystery being, of course, who were the builders of this and the other cities, towns, and villages of the Indus Valley; where did they come from; and why did their empire which stretched no less than 1,000 miles from the Simla Hills to the Arabian Sea collapse and disappear as though it had never existed?

The traveller will surely ask himself these questions as he gazes at the Citadel which dominated the city itself, as medieval castles towered above the communities they protected. These people, he will say, knew how to build, for even after nearly 5,000 years their watch-towers are still standing. And they knew, too, how to make for themselves a comfortable as well as a secure life, for the Citadel includes a huge bath – or perhaps a swimming tank – thirty-nine feet long, twenty-three feet wide, and eight feet deep together with rows of smaller bathrooms, no doubt for the use of the garrison officers or the priests, who, as in all these protohistoric societies, were undoubtedly the secular as well as the spiritual rulers of the city.

Perhaps even more interesting than the great public buildings which prove by their size and construction how prosperous Mohenjo-Daro was in its heyday is the town-planning based on a system also found at Harappa 350 miles to the north. The system is that used in all modern cities: namely, a gridiron of main streets running north and south and crossed by those running east and west, dividing the city into rectangular blocks in the manner of an American metropolis. It is obvious that this sort of logical and efficient town-planning has to be carefully worked out and approved in advance, which strongly suggests that Mohenjo-Daro could not have grown up and expanded as London or any of the European capitals did – that is, haphazardly over a long period of time. Rather, it seems to have been laid out much as new cities were laid out by Roman army engineers all over Europe, Asia, and Africa; or, to go back to even earlier times, as towns were planned by the Etruscans and Phoenicians whose priest-kings first marked off an auspicious site and whose builders then completed the construction of the city on a gridiron system.

It is admittedly difficult to comprehend how this was, or could be, done without very superior leadership, trained architects, and skilled masons. But we simply have to admit on examining the ruins of Mohenjo-Daro that such were the designers and builders of that city. The more we examine the actual residence of the citizens, the more we are conscious of the modernity of their life-style. Certainly they were far in advance of, say, medieval European communities in their knowledge and usage of baths, lavatories, drains, and sewers. Indeed, it is really a little startling to see a western-type latrine some 5,000 years old, complete with an effluent channel passing through the wall into a pottery receptacle or a brick drain joined to the main sewer running under the street, especially in view of the squalor of the typical Asiatic slum.

So what does all this tell us of the inhabitants of Mohenjo-Daro and the people of the Indus civilization? A great deal, for we can at least guess how they lived in these two-storey houses with their windowless façades, almost identical in design to the homes in which only very wealthy families in Pakistan live to-day. The Mohenjo-Daro house was built round a main courtyard, with the principal rooms facing inwards on to an open area around which the family sat in the cool of the evening. Within the house itself, the facilities included a dining-room, kitchen, a bathroom floored with carefully laid bricks, a well, pipes to carry off waste water including rain water from the roof, staircases, and a network of drains connected with the municipal sewage system. The city was not, of course, merely a residential area, but a working centre for merchants and craftsmen. In traditional oriental fashion, the specialist workmen like potters, weavers, jewellers, and others set up their workshops in prescribed districts of the city. Their output was large and trade extensive. The merchants of Mohenjo-Daro, in fact, seem to have been the principal brokers of international commerce, processing the raw materials from the Far East for trans-shipment to the Mesopotamian cities and handling imports from the West. Mohenjo-Daro and its sister-city Harappa were half-way houses for trade.

All these activities with the wealth and prosperity they engendered were made possible by the efficiency of a political system which, judging by the regimes in contemporary Egypt and Sumer, would be led by hierarchs, or priest-kings. In any case, all pre-classical civilizations were of this type – that is, theocracies in which the priests, as the guardians of the mysteries, were accepted as the indisputable rulers; and under their jurisdiction, while life in the Valley was highly civilized for this remote period, it must at the same time have been regimented and almost completely static. As far as we know, the culture of the Indus Valley scarcely changed or evolved at all over 1,000 years, implying strict conformity in the thinking and attitudes of all classes of citizens. At least, we assume this was so on analogy with such regimes as the Babylonians, but more especially in view of the conservatism of the script which seems not to have developed at all.

What, then, is this script? Was it invented by the people who built these forgotten cities? Is it related to any other script or language?

The answer to all these and related questions about the origin and nature of the written language of the Indus Valley is that we do not know. And yet we desperately need to know, since language and literature are the key to a people's mind; and so long as we are deprived of that key, we can never expect them to *speak* to us, however much archaeology tells us about how they laid out their cities, built their houses, and even clothed and adorned themselves. The citizens of ancient Athens and Rome, and, yes, even of Sumer and Babylon, communicate directly with any man or woman now living who cares to listen: we can hear their thoughts by reading their writing. The people of Mohenjo-Daro remain silent as well as faceless despite a few bronze statuettes and terracotta figurines unearthed from their buried homes and tombs. We cannot decipher the written messages they have left us.

The Indus Valley script consists of 396 different characters discovered on some 1,000 steatite or soapstone seals. Irrespective of the writing on them, these seals are themselves of a very high artistic order, and they are all the more precious since without them and a few score figurines, we have no aesthetic contact whatsoever with the people of the Indus Valley. The seals, then, are the nearest artefacts we have to pictures for many of the signs found on them are unmistakably pictographs, like the stylized drawings of men and animals. Sometimes the man-figure is carrying a weapon, sometimes an implement. The sign of a man with a bow, for instance, must surely denote a *soldier*, as that of a bold vertical stroke with a cluster of thinner strokes springing from its top signifies a *tree*.

But a pictographic script is not, of course, as simple as that. A sign that begins as a *star* ends by meaning a *king*, as in the Sumerian script. Moreover, the majority of the Mohenjo-Daro signs are not plain pictographs, but have become ideographs like our own sign + which can be *read* as 'plus' or 'in addition to'. We still use a number of such ideographs in English and seem to be using more and more of them as literacy becomes less important. But the difficulty in deciphering this Indus Valley script is two-fold: first, what texts we have are written on seals containing on an average some half a dozen letters; and secondly, it seems probable that the writing on these seals was simply for identification, as the writing on English coins reading D.G.REG.F.D.Elizabeth II[1] is for the purposes

---

1. Dei Gratia Regina Fidei Defenstrix Elizabeth Secunda.

of conformity. But obviously such signs and symbols give us no clue as to the language itself or to the grammatical structure, and all we can do until we discover a longer, or better a bilingual, text is to guess at the significance of the pictographs.

As with other 'mystery' languages – Etruscan is the classical example – cryptographers have spent countless hours poring over the Indus Valley seals, but few, surprisingly enough, have claimed to have solved the enigma. Colonel Lawrence Austine Waddell, a professor of, among things, Tibetan and the inventor of such theories as the Aryan origin of the alphabet and the Phoenician origin of the Britons, wrote a book in 1925 professing to have deciphered what he calls 'the Indo-Sumerian language as spoken by the Phoenicians, Barats, Goths, and Vedic Aryans'. The colonel states that within a day or two of receiving photographs of the Mohenjo-Daro seals, he was able to decipher and read the greater part of the inscriptions. Unfortunately for most of us his translations are as mysterious as the original. This is his translation of Seal No XIII:

O Setting-Sun Fish! the sage Uggu the God lift up from grave, bring to life, at Edin.[1]

The 'Setting-Sun Fish', we are told, is a translation of the Sumerian word *Pish*, while 'Uggu' or Hugo refers to the maternal uncle of Panek, the Phoenician prince. Alas! we are not much the wiser.

Another theory was suggested by M. G. de Hevesy at a meeting on 22 June 1933 of the Société Préhistorique Française to the effect that the language and script of Mohenjo-

1. L. A. Waddell, *The Indo-Sumerian Seals Deciphered*, London: Luzac, 1925, p 81.

Daro had a common origin with that of Easter Island. Using the rare wooden tablets known as *rongo-rongo*, de Hevesy produced a comparative table of the signs employed by the two scripts and sought to demonstrate an unmistakable resemblance between a hundred signs, including twenty of men holding weapons or various implements. De Hevesy then went on to argue that the language of the Indus Valley and of Easter Island originated in East Asia, perhaps China, and came to both places by way of Polynesian explorer-colonists. It is hardly necessary to say that orthodox philologists refuse even to discuss this theory.[1]

But for those not beholden to orthodoxy, the French researcher's suggestions are at least stimulating, for we are now reasonably sure that the Easter Island script was not writing in our sense, but a system of mnemonics or memory-aids whereby a speaker glances at his 'notes' and then, his memory refreshed, tells his story. Such pictographs are a simple method of recording a man's name, title, and profession, and hence the frequent occurrence in both the Easter Island *rongo-rongos* and the Mohenjo-Daro seals of stylized drawings of men with weapons or implements, placed next to other signs which appear to be ideographs. But it is now generally agreed that such writings found on seals consists of short informative statements like those found on modern identity documents, say passports and driving licences. Again, the great number of seals found in the houses of Mohenjo-Daro and Harappa suggest that the head of every family was required to carry an 'identification disc', giving his name, patronymic, and title or profession, thus: A, son of B, mason.

But so far all is guesswork. Nobody, for instance, knows what precisely was the significance of the animals which

---

[1]. M. G. de Hevesy, 'Sur une écriture océanienne', *Bulletin de la Société Préhistorique Française* (1933), Nos 7–8.

appear on almost every seal, the most common being a bull. Other animals depicted are either real or mythical: e.g. rhinoceroses, elephants, and crocodiles, on the one hand; and anthropomorphic monsters on the other. These creatures are invariably shown standing beside what appears to be either a small manger, or a vessel intended to receive the blood of the sacrificed animal. Whatever the interpretation, it is certain that the bull was an official emblem of state, comparable with our own heraldic insignia – the crowned lion of the British coat of arms, or the spread-winged eagle of the Great Seal of the United States. Certainly there is something ritualistic about these magnificent bulls which give the impression that they are connected with the national religion. But what this religion was, little that is meaningful in the present state of our knowledge can be said. To begin with, it is extremely difficult for people brought up in a twentieth-century industrialized society to comprehend the force of religion in an agrarian theocracy. So perhaps it is delusory to speculate on the significance of these 'sacred' bulls standing over their mangers, or the inner meaning of the terrocotta figurines of naked girls, or the function of the phallus-like stones (some over two feet in length) found in the ruins. The jargon of the anthropologists – fertility rites, Earth Mother, and so forth – does not really answer our questions.

What is more certain is that the priest-kings who ruled Mohenjo-Daro and Harappa were powerless to prevent their gradual decline. Now it is possible that this decline was due to natural calamities like earthquakes, floods, and the shifting of the waterways. On the other hand, a people that had built up these great cities, had colonized tens of thousands of square miles of north-west India, and had commercial relations with the contemporary city-states across the sea were surely capable of overcoming such seasonal disasters, particularly as they apparently had no enemies in the shape of rival states.

There seem, then, to have been other causes for the disintegration of this rich and prosperous civilization, and some historians suggest that Harappa, Mohenjo-Daro, and their satellite towns and villages were overthrown in a series of invasions by the Aryans sometime in the second millennium BC. From what we know of these Aryans – and that is very little indeed – they must be counted barbarians in comparison with the people they invaded. The vague literary sources available to us in the Vedic hymns give a picture of a tribal folk who lived for war (meaning, of course, raiding and looting), which they waged from two-horsed, two-wheeled chariots. Their arms were bows and spears. Actually this description tells us little, since it could apply to all protohistoric Euro-Asian tribes, all of whom are portrayed as mighty axe men, gargantuan eaters, and great drinkers: in short, a warrior aristocracy quite familiar to us from our own Old English sagas.

The only defence against such fierce and ruthless adversaries was not simply the strength of a city's walls, but the discipline of its citizens; and no enemy force, however numerous or reckless, could have breached the huge fortifications of Mohenjo-Daro in its heyday, if it had been properly defended by a loyal and well-trained militia. The conquest and sacking of the city suggest that in the end the old order imposed by the hierarchs had broken down, for reasons we do not and cannot know. But the breakdown of law and order is invariably reflected in the deterioration of the physical aspects of cities – the neglect of roads, the construction of gimcrack buildings, and the increase of slum housing. Archaeologists have shown, for instance, that the Great Granary of Mohenjo-Daro was used in the end to house what were probably paupers – citizens who had no definite trade or function and had to be supported by the state. As these increased in number, standards of living declined; and even more significant, the corporate will to overcome disasters and resist enemies grew weaker. It would appear from the number of corpses left sprawling about where they were murdered that when the barbarians came (as they must always have been waiting to come), they met with scant opposition. The archaeologist Ernest Mackay reports that he found a group of nine skeletons, amongst them five children, huddled together in strangely contorted attitudes.[1] They had obviously been struck down without mercy. And elsewhere in the ruins other skeletons revealed that the city could not have been defended at all in the end, for the bandits merely walked in and murdered people in the streets, like the family of four on their way to a well. And so violence followed physical decay, until the entire system seems to have collapsed and Mohenjo-Daro, Harappa, and the scores of other Indus Valley communities were no more. A civilization had died. But we still find it strange that the great cities of this particular empire should have disappeared without a trace, and without a clue as to what they were called and who built them, except, as we have seen, for a handful of artefacts which speak to us if not in the language of scholarship, then in that of the senses. The little dancer of Mohenjo-Daro with her score of bracelets all the way up one arm while the other rests on her hip speaks louder than the massive walls of the Citadel. And it is no use the pedants muttering the incantation, 'Mother goddess! Fertility rites!' That is not what we hear her saying.

1. Ernest John Henry Mackay, *The Indus Civilization*, London: L. Dickson & Thompson, 1935, p 185.

Angkor

From Mohenjo-Daro in Pakistan to Angkor in Cambodia – a journey of nearly 2,000 miles . . . Is there any link between these two capitals of civilizations so widely separated in both space and time? A tentatively affirmative answer is suggested by one small artefact unearthed from the Indus Valley site. It is one of those mysterious seals, and it portrays a figure in a horned head-dress, his arms laden with bangles, and his knees spread apart in a squatting posture so characteristic of Asia, so alien to the West. This ithyphallic personage is generally thought to be the progenitor of one of the principal gods of India – Shiva. It is Shiva who reappears 2,000 miles and 2,000 years away in the middle of the Cambodian jungle. For the complex of temples that are known collectively as Angkor were partially inspired by veneration of this Indian god.

A strange deity, stranger even than his compères, Maya and Vishnu, who complete the Brahman-Hindu trinity, the former with his four heads and four arms, mounted on a goose; the latter, a man-lion who tears out the entrails of his human prey laid across his knees. But Shiva manages to be even more bizarre, for it was this member of the sacred triad who decapitated his son in a fit of rage and then, on the plea of his wife, replaced the severed cranium with the head of an elephant. It is not surprising that a god capable of this degree of eccentricity was worshipped in the form of a phallus, first at Mohenjo-Daro where his typical stone lingas have been found and 3,000 years later at Angkor.

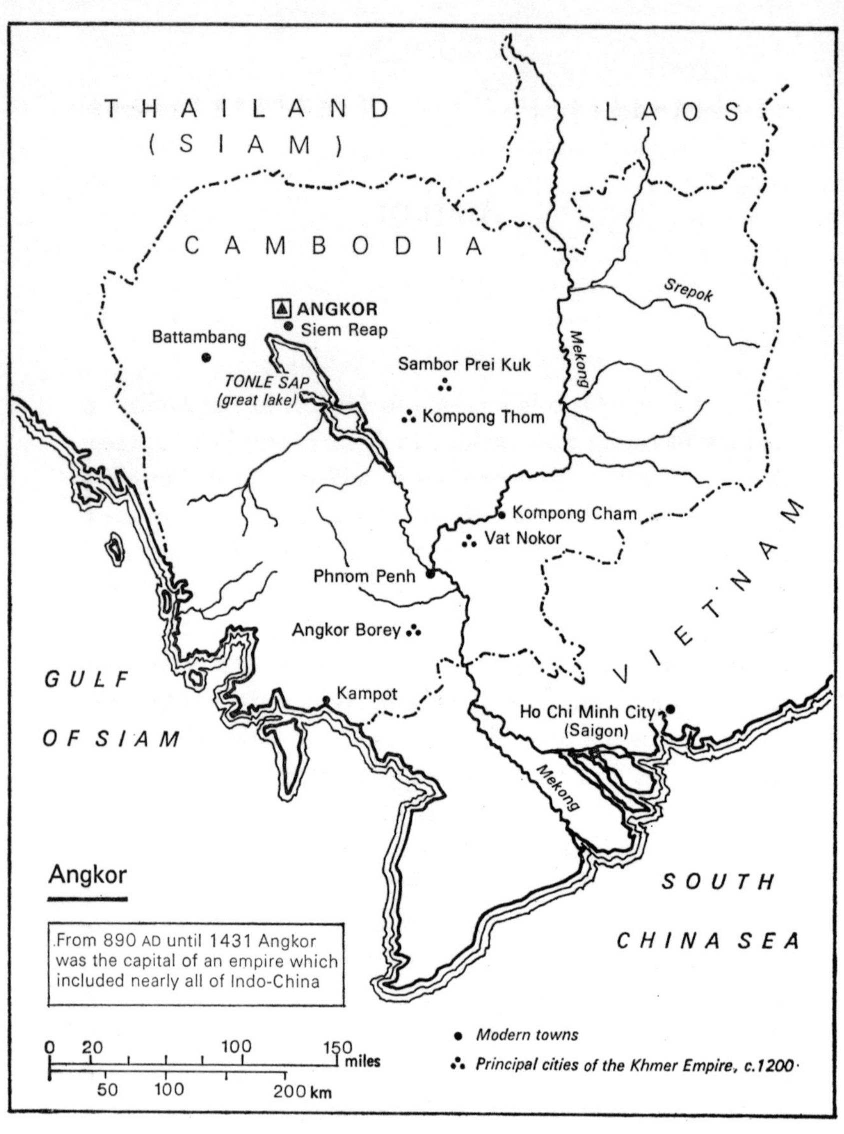

THAILAND
(SIAM)
LAOS
CAMBODIA
Srepok
ANGKOR
Siem Reap
Battambang
Sambor Prei Kuk
TONLE SAP
(great lake)
Kompong Thom
Mekong
Kompong Cham
Vat Nokor
Phnom Penh
VIETNAM
Angkor Borey
GULF
OF SIAM
Kampot
Ho Chi Minh City
(Saigon)
Mekong
SOUTH
CHINA SEA
Angkor
.From 890 AD until 1431 Angkor
was the capital of an empire which
included nearly all of Indo-China
0   20   100   150
                              miles
    50   100   200 km
Modern towns
Principal cities of the Khmer Empire, c.1200

But here the connection between the two cities ends, for Mohenjo-Daro, despite being so much older than Angkor, strikes the visitor as being the more 'modern' of the two; and the reason is that the Indus Valley metropolis was obviously a commercial emporium comparable with a well-laid out and functional American city, whereas the Cambodian capital was primarily a religious centre, comparable with such hierarchical townships as the Vatican of Rome and Lhasa in Tibet. Hence, when we speak of Angkor, we are referring in general to two large temple complexes within the city boundaries: Angkor Wat built in the twelfth century AD and Angkor Thom built in the eleventh.

There are several other temple sites which are also part of Angkor and still other characteristic monuments dotted all over the old Khmer empire which extended well beyond the present-day frontiers of Cambodia. But Angkor, the royal capital from around AD 950 to 1431 when it was sacked by the Thai armies and virtually abandoned, was, and still remains, the history in stone of a nation until recently lost in obscurity.

Incidentally, one of the very earliest visitors to Angkor seems to have been aware of the relationship between the gods of ancient India and those of medieval Cambodia. He was Chou Ta Kuen, a Chinese diplomat who spent a year in the capital in 1296; and his account of the city reveals that he was greatly intrigued by a people who venerated a deity in the guise of a penis and deified a king who mutilated all his brothers on his ascendancy to the throne by cutting off their toes. Chou Ta Kuen was not at all surprised that such a man chose the linga to symbolize the 'essence of his soul' and considered it his duty to sleep every night with a nine-headed snake.

Only after he has performed his duty with this celestial

spouse does he leave his bed-chamber to visit his wives and concubines.[1]

As he had five of the former (a principal wife and one for every cardinal point of the compass) and 3–5,000 of the latter, he must have been fully occupied, as the Chinese diplomat noted, particularly as the Cambodian women were 'very lascivious, though, because of continuous pregnancy, at twenty they resemble a Chinese woman of forty'.

So Chou Ta Kuen finds everything in Angkor as strange as we find the ruins of the city to-day, and implies that the inhabitants are not really quite right in the head and certainly not wholly civilized. While not unconditionally disapproving, he does deprecate such customs as the young women bathing naked in the river, since:

> Everybody can see them. Indeed, the Chinese residents go down to the river on their day off to witness this spectacle; and it is said that some go into the water in order to profit from the occasion.[2]

Whether Chou betook himself down to the river in order to 'witness the spectacle' or contrived to 'profit from the occasion', he manifestly regarded the Cambodians as semi-barbarians despite the size and splendour of their capital Angkor; and one must admit the word 'barbaric' seems apposite when Chou tells us that in the eighth month of the year the king required a huge amphora to be filled with thousands of gallbladders 'taken live from men hunted down in the forests by special

1. 'Sur les coûtumes de Cambodge de Tchou Ta-Kouan', translated by Paul Pelliot, *Bulletins de l'Ecole Française de l'Extrême Orient*, Tome 2, No 2 (Avril-Juin, 1902), p 145.

2. *op cit*, p 155.

squads armed with small knives with which they opened their victims' stomachs and cut out the spleen'. When enough gall-bladders had been collected to satisfy the royal wishes, the organs were expressed to yield the bile stored in the vesicular sac, each bladder yielding around 1.7 fluid ounces of liquid. This effusion, mixed with *eau de vie* to taste, was imbibed by the king, or used to wash the head of the royal elephant, the lavage being necessary in view of the pachyderm's refusal to drink this unusual brew. In both cases, the object was to increase the valour of man and beast. Chou obviously thought this was going a bit too far, though his own compatriots at a later time themselves introduced dried gallbladders into their pharmacopeia and obtained the necessary organs in the same manner as the Cambodians, as the Italian priest Father Filippo de Marini noted in 1660, adding that the hunters attacked women as well as men so great was the demand for human bile.

The Chinese diplomat tells us enough, then, to explain why we instinctively find Angkor and the other Khmer ruins so strange, an impression which even the French archaeologists who worked continuously for years at the sites admitted they could never quite escape. Pierre Loti who visited Angkor in 1909 epitomizes this impression in a memorable description:

> I looked up at the tree-covered towers which dwarfed me when all of a sudden my blood curdled as I saw an enormous smile looking down on me, and then another smile over on another wall, then three, then five, then ten, appearing from every direction. I was being observed from all sides.[1]

What are these stone faces which actually made a sea captain's blood curdle? Well, they are sometimes the portraits in stone

1. Pierre Loti, *Un Pèlerin d'Angkor*, Paris: Calmann-Levy, 1912, p 75.

of the reigning king, his wife, his parents, his grandparents, his sons, and occasionally friends and relations, and could it not be that all these faces are grinning for a very good reason – they have all been deified in life?

This, then, is the answer to the riddle which Angkor always posed to early travellers and continues to pose for the visitor to-day. We are looking at a city built not for the accommodation of men, but for the glorification of gods in their human form – that is, as god-kings. Whatever we see to-day – buildings, walls, statues – were all funerary monuments, never intended to serve the living, but to immortalize the dead. So Angkor is really a vast cemetery where the inhabitants lived among tombs. And this is the reason for the eerie aspect of the place. At whatever hour one visits the Bayon, the central temple of Angkor Thom, and especially by moonlight, the visitor is conscious of a sense of other-worldliness, almost as though the people who built it came from another planet. We know now, of course, where they did come from, that they were a people called the Khmers whose descendants still occupy the mountainous regions of Cambodia; but we still find their culture alien and mysterious, for the worship of sun-kings and snakes and phallic-shaped stones and lingas carved with human faces remains not only incomprehensible to the Western observer, but also either vaguely menacing or outright ludicrous. It was the former sensation to which Pierre Loti was referring: gigantic faces grinning down from each side of eighty towers can indeed cause a feeling of incredulity.

Nothing of this tenuous link between Mohenjo-Daro and Angkor was known to the French missionary who discovered the lost Cambodian city in 1850; and nothing could have been known, since the existence of both the Indus Valley civilization and the extent of the Khmer empire were unwritten chapters in the story of mankind. The first to relate the opening lines of that story was the missionary Father Charles-Émile Bouillevaux, who reached the city then deep in the jungle on foot. He tells us, in fact, that he walked over a mile and a half across the burning sand on bare feet and arrived '*dans un triste état*'. Perhaps this was why the Father was not over-impressed by what he had discovered in the middle of the Cambodian forest, though he admits that the principal temple he saw, which was the Bayon at Angkor Thom, impressed him as '*grandiose, magnifique, malgré sa bizarrerie*'.[1]

If Father Bouillevaux was not particularly interested in the massive and mysterious monuments which he was the first European to see, it is not hard to understand his seeming indifference when one realizes what an extraordinary and unknown country Cambodia was in 1850, a country full of ancient ruins hidden in impenetrable forests. Moreover, the missionaries sent out by the apostolic church were naturally more concerned with the people they had come to save than they were in the tombs of their ancestors; and in any case Father Bouillevaux's time and energy during his sojourn in Cambodia were principally occupied in making a friend and ally of His Majesty Ong Duong, a business which left him with little time to explore the ruins of pagan temples. For King Ong Duong was a monarch to be treated with great tact. He had, in fact, just returned from captivity in Siam where he had kept himself alive by his skill in repairing the watches and clocks of his captors; and he was not in the least interested in his country's antiquities. On the contrary, he was far more concerned in keeping abreast with European technology, and his house was full of cheap gewgaws from European manufactories. The priest did not altogether trust this 'grown-up

1. C. E. Bouillevaux, *Voyage dans L'Indo-Chine, 1848–1856*, Paris: Victor Palme, 1858, pp242 ff.

chi!d', as he calls the monarch, more especially when he was served eau-de-Cologne at dinner and pressed to drink it on the grounds that this toilet-water was a European wine. One of the guests who did drink it out of fear for his royal host passed out on the spot and was only revived with great difficulty.

However, Father Bouillevaux did eventually visit the ruined city of Angkor, but apparently only because the King was alarmed by his, the missionary's, pallor which he informs us was not so much a pallor as a greenish hue, the result of a year and a half's incarceration in a windowless hut in Cochin China. And so for his visit to the temples, Father Bouillevaux was provided with a miniature horse, on to which he leapt in an attempt to show that he was not as feeble as he looked, only to fly right over the animal's head, nearly, as he says, 'breaking his back'. But off the missionary went, followed by a group of local Cambodians and their dogs, until after an hour they came to three hills in the middle of the plain, and here he saw the tombs of the ancient kings, and all around enormous walls and huge brick buildings. He was struck by the stature of a seated Buddha forty feet in height – 'I have never before seen such a monster'. But as for the architecture in general, 'there was nothing very remarkable about it, for everything was in ruins'. The site was a veritable city of the dead where 'the tiger roams around the crumbling walls at night and the snake makes his nest in the tombs.'[1] He was, however, impressed by the statue of the 'Leper King', a remarkable sculpture of some still unidentified Cambodian god seated on the ground with one leg akimbo, the arms and legs covered with a lichen which gives the appearance of leprosy. Since he had seen the 'Leper King', as this statue continues to be called, he must have passed the Terrace of the Elephants and wandered about the temple

1. *op cit*, p 169, 170.

complex of Angkor Thom. The good Father sums up his impressions of the Cambodia of 130 years ago in these words: 'The Orient to-day has been lulled to sleep in idleness and pleasure, and no longer counts in our time; the ancient Orient is a mysterious lost world of priestly ritual and vast ruins'.[1]

Father Bouillevaux was followed by the French naturalist Henri Mouhot who reached the capital of the Khmer empire in 1858, eight years after the missionary. Mouhot was a very different type of explorer from his predecessor, so much so that his account of the ruins almost seems to be of another place altogether, which is probably why he is often credited with being the discoverer of Angkor. The young naturalist (he was only twenty-four when he set out on his travels through Indo-China) was enormously enthusiastic about everything he saw and is quite lyrical on the magnificence of the Angkor temples, one of which, he contends, 'is grander than anything left us by Greece or Rome'.[2] This, of course, was a very large claim to make in an age in which nearly all aesthetic taste was regulated by classical norms, but one which Mouhot did his best to justify by his descriptions and drawings. Indeed the illustrations of the main temple of Angkor Wat show how relatively intact were the buildings which he surveyed, measured, and described. For typical of Victorian travellers, he was a man of many talents, able to record whatever he saw in words and pictures and, just as important an attribute for travellers in the unexplored regions of Asia and Africa, able to endure dangers and hardships with courage and patience. And so Henri Mouhot set about measuring and

1. *op cit*, p 242. Translation by James Wellard.
2. Henri Mouhot, *Travels in the Central Parts of Indo-China during the years 1858, 1859, and 1860*, London: Murray, 1864, pp 268, 269.

counting and sketching as much of the great complex at Angkor as he could reach, while trying to penetrate the mystery of such a splendid city lost to Western history and not even known about by the descendants of the builders themselves. For all the local villagers could tell the explorer about Angkor was that 'it is the work of giants', a statement with which, he says, he agrees. Even so, he was extremely anxious to know the true human history of Angkor, but in the end, having no firm clue of its occupants, could only guess that it was built more than 2,000 years ago. The young traveller was never to learn more about the ruins, for shortly afterwards during his journey from Bangkok to Laos he fell sick of 'the fever' and again, typical of his generation, insisted on pressing on to his destination, all the while making careful notes of everything *en route*, including the latitude and longitude of important centres and, of course, the daily noon temperature, which always seemed to be significant to the early explorers. But his notes get shorter and shorter, and the last three entries tell the whole story of his sufferings and of his end:

18th October [1860] Halted at H.
19th   Attacked by fever
29th   Have pity on me, O my God . . .[1]

Mouhot's *Travels* was published posthumously in 1864 and the book at once aroused great interest in French historical and archaeological circles, especially since by this time Cambodia had become a French protectorate, which meant that exploration could now be conducted in comparative safety under the aegis of the army; and it was not long before properly equipped expeditions were visiting Angkor and submitting their reports to learned societies back in Europe. In 1898 the

1. *op cit*, vol ii, p 160.

École Française de l'Extrême Orient had been instituted and, very soon afterwards a complete inventory of Cambodian monuments was issued, together with a translation of many of the inscriptions which immediately clarified the religious and political annals of the Khmer Empire and made it part of universal history. The continuous efforts of French archaeologists and scholars have almost completed the story of Angkor.

But when we say this, we are really only saying that we can now date most of the monuments within a few score years; that we know the names of many kings and the duration of their reigns; and that we have discovered the reason for the construction of so many temples. But as for the everyday life of the people who inhabited the capital cities of the god-kings, we know very little – even less than we know of societies thousands of years older. For in certain respects, Angkor, like Mohenjo-Daro in Pakistan and Copán in Honduras, eludes us, however meticulously these three cities are dug over. Angkor, for instance, astounds, even mesmerizes, us with its temples and tombs, but its immense public works – roads, bridges, reservoirs, and rest-houses – which prove that commerce was at the heart of the empire's prosperity are hardly ever mentioned in the standard guidebooks, for we have no records of these vital activities. The same criticism is true of Copán, as we shall see, so that to this extent, the picture of these cities – and, in particular, of the people who inhabited them – is distorted, for when we assert that Angkor, Mohenjo-Daro, and Copán were the capitals of theocentric states, we are in danger of assuming that the ordinary citizen spent his entire time in building temples and worshipping the gods. We do not, in fact, know, since without some sort of profane literature, or even much in the way of popular art, we have absolutely no way of entering into the lives, and certainly not the thoughts, of these long-dead Cambodians; and the nearest we shall ever get to knowing something about these people are those little anecdotes and occasional observations of the Chinese diplomat Chou Ta Kuen. Chou gives us, for instance, little snippets of information implying that the ordinary people seemed to him ugly and very dark, and only the royal personages and the wives of nobles were as white as jade, on account of the sun never touching them. Slaves and servants imported from the mountain fastnesses were regarded as outside the human race. They were always obliged to approach their masters and mistresses on hands and knees and when beaten were not allowed to move.

From such descriptions we begin to glimpse something of the day-to-day life of the people, though even here, about all we are really told is that the nobility did nothing and the slaves were their churls. We still know nothing of the free craftsmen and farmers who, in the final analysis, must have kept the whole edifice standing.

We can assume from analogies with other societies dependent upon slave labour that the magnificent temples and the extensive public works could not have been built without the effort of hordes of human robots, though the architects and master-craftsmen were presumably free men and undoubtedly artists of genius. The designer of such a temple as the Banteay Srei, the tiny 'citadel of women' finely carved in pink sandstone, was such a man, and so was the sculptor of the 'Leper King'.

At the same time, both architects and sculptors throughout the imperial days of Cambodia – from the eighth to the fifteenth centuries – were conditioned, rather than inspired, by the concepts of a wholly theocratic state. In such societies, all art is religious in a broad sense; and every object that we see in Angkor is of this kind, including the quasi-erotic sculptures of the dancing-girls on the walls of Angkor Wat. But while the sculptors had a certain amount of latitude, the architects

The great elliptical structure of the 'Temple' at Zimbabwe gave
rise to many theories as to its origin: among them, that it was
built by the same Sabaeans who built at Marib

The Conical Tower at Zimbabwe is 30 ft high, 8 ft in diameter at the top, and is solidly built. Most explorers connected it with phallic worship, but its origins and purpose are unknown

had very little. Each Cambodian temple is designed to a specific plan which allows no variation in the essential lay-out of a building. For very simply, the intention was to reproduce not a church or a palace, but a microcosm of the Hindu-Buddhist Universe. Thus the plan of Angkor Wat, Angkor Thom, the Bayon, and other complexes begins with the idea of the mountain called Meru, the centre of the universe and the abode of the gods. This magic mountain was represented in the Cambodian capital at Angkor by the central temple, while the foothills surrounding Meru were reproduced as the encircling walls, with the ocean beyond represented by the moat. This design is referred to in a stele dating from around AD 1060 which specifically states that the King, Udayadityavarman II, thought it fitting to have the representation of Meru in the centre of the capital he was building at Angkor Thom. What we are seeing at Angkor, then, is not merely a city, but a microcosm of a mythological universe; and the function of a city of this nature was not to house men, but to accommodate the gods. For this reason the towers of the central temple reach upwards to the heavens and symbolize the 'gateway to the sky', precisely as the Babylonian ziggurats and Christian cathedrals reach upwards as if to proclaim in stone man's spiritual yearning to touch heaven itself.

Once the visitor to Angkor is familiar with this cosmogony of the three Indian religions, Brahmanism, Hinduism, and Buddhism, the plan and meaning of the capital become clear. It was literally built as a city of god, and nothing was designed or constructed for the objectives for which we build our cities – for utilitarian purposes tempered (if we are lucky) with aesthetic considerations. Perhaps the best examples we have of this view of urban planning are seen in the now-desecrated Georgian squares of London. But at Angkor the visitor is really looking at tombs, not palaces, since the Cambodian kings, like the Pharaohs, started to build their funeral monuments while alive and erected larger and more imposing monuments according to the importance of the person to be commemorated. In the case of the later kings, the central temples which, as we have seen, symbolized Mount Meru, the home of the gods, became the personal and private shrine of the monarch who, by his communication with Vishnu or Shiva or Buddha, himself became divine even before he was dead. Thus King Surayvarman II who reigned during the first half of the twelfth century, built himself the special mausoleum or sanctuary of Angkor Wat wherein he dwelt in the manner of Vishnu with whom he identified himself. We get hints from Chou Ta Kuen of the peculiar existence of such a god-king, though there were departures from his divine isolation from mortal affairs in some of the activities in which his mirror-self, Vishnu, indulged, activities demonstrated in the carvings of the graceful *apsaras* or celestial 'call-girls', expert in delighting even a god like Vishnu, who seems to have tried everything, including a bout of cannibalism. No doubt the 3–5,000 concubines mentioned by Chou were the living representatives of these graceful nymphs we see portrayed on the walls of Angkor Wat, all of them housed in the environs of the royal palace. But how all these women lived or passed their time we have no way of knowing, since nothing of either the king's residence or the homes of any of his subjects has survived, all domestic structures being built of wood as stone was restricted to religious buildings.

If it were not for the rather droll account left by Chou Ta Kuen, one would have to assume on the evidence of the monuments and inscriptions found by the École Française de l'Extrême Orient during fifty years of excavations that Angkor was actually a vast tomb or complex of tombs built by royal megalomaniacs, whose entire earthly existence revolved around their desire to become gods. Such an obsession, even in an Oriental king, strikes us as so irrational that even the

most informed visitor finds these Cambodian temples, even
when cleared of their jungle covering, inexpressibly puzzling.
No other lost city in the world – not even Petra – evokes
instantaneously and instinctively this sense of eeriness eman-
ating from the Bayon monument of Angkor Thom, for instance, with its cluster of forty-nine ornate towers, each having
a gigantic face carved on each of its four sides, a total of 196
monstrous heads rising higher and higher into the sky.
Even when we know that these faces are only the *numina* of
the ever-watchful and omnipresent god-king Jayavarman VII
who reigned from 1181 to *circa* 1210 and who, in life, was a
little plump man with a pleasant, bland countenance, the powerful magic of the Bayon still persists. The explanation is that we
are in the presence of religious and architectural creations that
some find irrational, some wholly absurd.

But whatever the aesthetic verdict on the forty-nine towers
and 196 grinning faces of Jayavarman, history makes it clear
that this god-king ended by ruining his country with the most
extravagant and wasteful programme of building ever undertaken by a tyrant. For in addition to erecting Angkor Thom
as his mausoleum wherein he would be immortalized as Jaya-
Buddha during his lifetime, this monarch constructed many
provincial sanctuaries together with hundreds of rest-houses
and hospitals, all dedicated to his own apotheosis; and all of
these projects, which were enormously expensive to build and
maintain, were made possible only by the ruthless taxation of
free citizens and the enforced labour of slaves. In short, almost
the entire resources of the nation were expended on a programme of building shrines and sanctuaries, of staffing them
with hundreds of thousands of monks, of feeding an enormous
army of slaves and servitors, and of furnishing the temples
with golden idols for the self-glorification of one man. Jayavarman had managed to create a welfare state for the priests paid
for by the workers. It is scarcely surprising that such a system

which pampered the idle and impoverished the industrious collapsed at the first sign of opposition. During the war with the neighbouring Siamese, the people who had been forced to do all the work were now forced to do the fighting to protect the temples, shrines, and sanctuaries they did not want. Apparently they had had enough of god-kings, for about now in the middle of the twelfth century, the great and extensive Khmer empire began to disintegrate, and by 1432 the capital Angkor was abandoned. Within a few decades, it had actually disappeared under the foliage of giant trees.

This was how Father Bouillevaux saw the site in 1850, and it is only fitting that he, as the discoverer of Angkor, should have the last word:

Entering the forest, I turned towards the ancient city, formerly the residence of the kings. As soon as I had climbed over the ramparts, I discovered some immense ruins which I was told were the site of the royal palace. On the walls which were carved from top to bottom I saw combats between elephants, men fighting with clubs and spears, and others firing three arrows at a time from their bows. The interior of the ancient city is full of ruins. But now a dense forest covers them all and enormous trees grow right out of the ruined palaces . . .

There are few sensations sadder than seeing lost and deserted cities which were once the scenes of glory and pleasure. And as later in the day I watched the sun go down behind the great trees of the forest, I compared the shades of night which were blotting out the landscape with the life of nations deprived of fame and hope.[1]

1. *op cit*, pp 245, 6.

Part 3
Africa

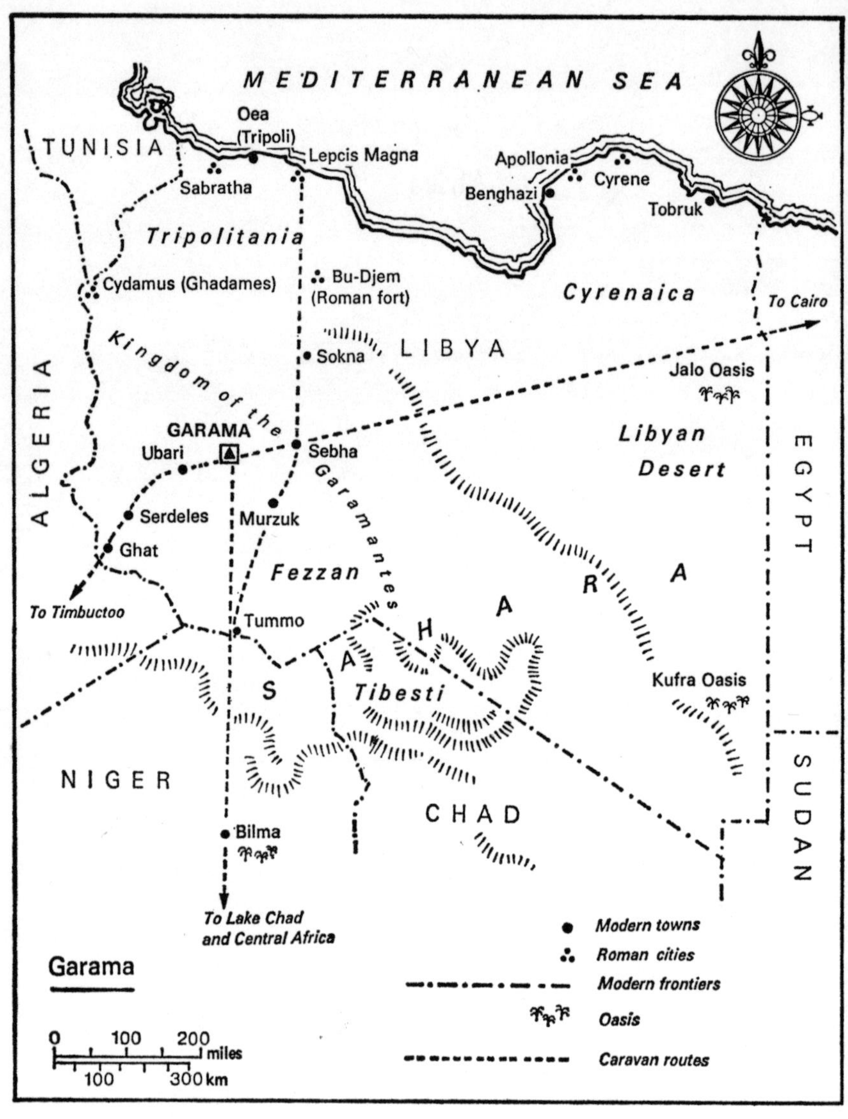

MEDITERRANEAN SEA
TUNISIA
Oea (Tripoli)
Sabratha
Lepcis Magna
Apollonia
Cyrene
Benghazi
Tobruk
Tripolitania
Cyrenaica
Cydamus (Ghadames)
Bu-Djem (Roman fort)
Kingdom of the
LIBYA
Sokna
Jalo Oasis
To Cairo
Libyan Desert
GARAMA
Ubari
Sebha
EGYPT
Serdeles
Murzuk
Garamantes
Ghat
Fezzan
To Timbuctoo
Tummo
S   A   H   A   R   A
Kufra Oasis
Tibesti
NIGER
SUDAN
CHAD
Bilma
To Lake Chad
and Central Africa
Modern towns
Roman cities
Modern frontiers
Oasis
Caravan routes
Garama
0   100   200   miles
100   300 km

Garama

To the Sahara Desert and the southernmost frontier of the Roman Empire! Our destination, Garama, 'a most renowned city' according to Pliny; capital of 'an exceedingly great nation' according to Herodotus. The traveller to-day who manages to reach Garama, which is now buried beneath a scorpion-infested and abandoned oasis called Germa in the Fezzan province of Libya, may find it difficult to believe either historian. While both men, the Roman and the Greek, had visited Africa, neither had got as far down as the Fezzan and certainly had not set foot in Garama. Indeed, until quite recently it was still something of an adventure to travel any-where in southern Libya, and not many explorers have actually seen the site of Garama since the Roman commander Cornelius Balbus led an expedition against the Garamantes and captured their capital in 20 BC.

My first chance to visit Pliny's 'renowned city' came in 1965 when Libya was a kingdom reigned over by a benign old gentleman called Sayyid Idris and foreigners came and went as they pleased, except that few travellers, apart from the ubiquit-ous oil-men, were interested in this former Italian colony. The capital Tripoli in those days was much as the old Turkish beys had left it, and once away from the ugly concrete structures run up by the Fascists, it was not all that difficult to imagine the town as it had been in the days of Barbarossa. Eighty miles to the east lay the most splendid city of Roman Africa, Lepcis Magna; and a unique experience it was to visit this once-thriving port and to wander, alone, through a metropolis which was the birthplace of an emperor. Indeed, Lepcis Magna where Septimius Severus was born and York where he died and Garama on the edge of the Sahara were all typical, each in its own way, of an empire that stretched from the Scottish Highlands to the sands of the Great Desert.

It was the last of these Roman outposts that I was bound for aboard a Libyan bus. The journey took two days and a night to get as far as Sebha, the capital of the Fezzan and the jumping-off place for travellers going south to the Chad or south-westwards to the Niger. I travelled in company with an undetermined number of hooded men and veiled women, one sheep, and a dozen hens. Occasionally our bus stopped at a collection of mud huts; then some of the passengers left us and disappeared across the sands *en route* to their villages. The end of the road for the rest of us was the market square in Sebha and for me a dilapidated inn which had been hastily run up to accommodate the oil prospectors and half-abandoned when no oil was found.

My problem now was to continue my journey farther into the desert, to reach the oasis of Germa. There was, of course, no public or private transport in Sebha. The best advice offered me was to await one of the trans-African lorries which occasionally came through on the way to the Chad. But I was not bound for the Chad, I said. In that case it was as God willed . . .

However, the police had a post at Sebha, and after much tea-drinking and the exchange of cigarettes, the captain of the station agreed to send me to Germa in an old army jeep. And so I crossed the sand sea.

As I approached the historic site and saw the palm trees which marked the oasis, I paid homage to the first Europeans to reach Garama 2,000 years after the Romans had conquered it – the British explorers Lieutenant Hugh Clapperton, RN and Dr Walter Oudney. True, these travellers did not realize the importance of their discovery, but their report that they had come across what seemed to be a Roman-built mausoleum near an oasis called *Germa* was the clue historians had been waiting for. It came in the form of an entry in Dr Oudney's journal:

Monday, June 17 [1822]. – We were conducted to-day by Sheikh Mustapha to examine a building, different, as he stated, from any in the country. When we arrived, we found to our satisfaction that it was a structure which had been erected by the Romans . . .

This building is about twelve feet high and eight broad. It is built of sandstone, well finished, and dug from the neighbouring hills. Its interior is solid and of small stones, cemented with mortar. It stands about three miles from Germa and a quarter of a mile from the foot of the mountain. It is either a tomb or an altar: those well acquainted with Roman architecture will easily determine which. The finding of a structure of these people proves, without doubt, their intercourse here . . . We were not able to learn from the old sheikh whether any old coins were found, or any building similar to this, in the vicinity. Was this the track merely of the Romans into the interior, or did they come to the valley for dates?

Scholars back in Europe now knew for certain that the 'renowned city' of Pliny and the 'great nation' of Herodotus were historically real and not just the invention of the mythmakers. Since the mausoleum was built of dressed stone, then, it was certainly Roman; Germa was obviously a variant of Garama; and the land of the mysterious people called the Garamantes had therefore been found.

The chance discovery not only of a lost city but of the

southern limits of the Roman empire in Africa was typical of nineteenth-century exploration. And the discoverers, too, were typical. Lieutenant Clapperton and Dr Walter Oudney were members of a three-man team which had volunteered in 1822 for the extremely dangerous assignment of exploring the negro kingdom of Central Africa which up to that time no European had ever visited.

Lieutenant Clapperton was the tenth child of twenty-one children, of little schooling, and apprenticed at thirteen as a cabin boy. His biographer adds: 'He was full of fun and during his stay in Labrador hunted with the Indians and nearly married one of their princesses. He had a noble figure; was six feet high and broad-chested. He suffered the amorous persecution of a rich African widow called Zuma who pursued him everywhere on a white horse and with bands of barbaric music.'

Dr Walter Oudney, Clapperton's companion, is described as: 'born of humble parents in Edinburgh where he picked up sufficient knowledge of medicine to become a surgeon's mate on board a man-of-war. Of middle stature and slight build, with a pale, grave face, he appears to have been very successful in his intercourse with the natives.'

The third member of the expedition, Major Dixon Denham, was a professional soldier who distinguished himself at the battle of Toulouse (1813) by carrying Sir James Douglas, commanding a Portuguese brigade, out of fire when that officer had lost his leg. Denham's adventures read, says his biographer, 'like a frenzied dream'.[1]

These were the men commissioned to explore Central Africa. The plan was for Major Denham to push southwards to Bornu and Lake Chad, while Lieutenant Clapperton and

---

1. *Dictionary of National Biography*, Oxford University Press, 1973. Vol IV, pp 372–4; Vol XIV, p 1248; and Vol V, pp 791–2.

Dr Oudney journeyed south-westwards to the Fezzan. Unfortunately the doctor was ill throughout this arduous caravan march. Suffering severely from ague and fever (i.e., malaria and dysentery), he was unable to keep anything down but an occasional cup of coffee, though he insisted on attending to the sick along the line of march. Most of the men he visited in the villages were seeking a remedy against impotence, the women against sterility. What the Scots doctor gave them in the way of medicine we are not told, but Clapperton reports that he was constantly cupping himself in the belief that this would cure his hacking cough. It did the doctor no good. On the morning of 12 January 1824, he tried to mount his camel, but there was the ghastliness of death in his countenance. He died without a struggle or a groan, and his companion buried him under an old mimosa tree a little beyond the southern gate of a Nigerian village called Katagum. The Arabs later destroyed his grave, saying that he was a 'Kafir', meaning an infidel.

This was the man who, though he is now forgotten and whose monograph entitled *Excursion to Westwards of Mourzouk* is no longer read, nonetheless changed the writing of history, for the Roman mausoleum which he discovered near Germa has since become a landmark in the archaeology of the Roman world. The monument itself is still there, standing in the shadow of the rocky escarpment which runs along the length of the most historic valley in the Sahara desert, the Wadi el Ajal. It is a landscape which has not changed in thousands of years and looked the same to the Roman general Cornelius Balbus and the Scottish explorer Walter Oudney as it does to us. Even so, Oudney would be surprised if he could visit the Wadi el Ajal to-day. For not far away from his mausoleum he would find tangible evidence that the capital of Herodotus's 'exceeding great nation' lay beneath the mud huts of the oasis of Germa.

Without the knowledge painstakingly acquired by a handful

of scholars within the last few decades, it is admittedly difficult to comprehend the significance of Oudney's discovery. To begin with, the Wadi el Ajal, the main highway between Central Africa and the Mediterranean during the period of the Garamantes (500 BC(?)–AD 600) is now deserted save for a few nomads with their camels. Yet we know, and can see for ourselves, that this valley has been occupied continuously for the last 10,000 years, from prehistoric times when a race of hunters incised the rock-faces with pictures of animals that no longer inhabit this region to within living memory when Italian engineers built desert forts of the Foreign Legion type. In between, came herdsmen who displaced the primeval hunters; the Garamantes who invaded the region; the Romans who made treaties of alliance with the Garamantian kings; the Arabs who conquered them; the Tuareg who took over the valley as caravaners; and the Turks who built large straggling fortresses along the desert highway. Even so, while nearly all the Sahara has been explored and mapped, both from the land and the air, the country of the Garamantes remains virtually unknown; and their capital Garama still lies buried under a jumble of mud huts. It is an eerie place and difficult to believe that it once heard the trumpets and saw the banners of a Roman legion.

One reason for the obscurity of Garama is that the Fezzan has always been very much off the beaten track; and these days foreigners are not encouraged to wander freely about Libya. Another is that so far the archaeologists have never had the opportunity to do more than scrape the surface of the layers of lost civilizations which once flourished in this region of the Sahara. The best and most comprehensive work was done by the Italians during their occupation of Libya, and we must be deeply grateful to their scholars who produced for us the classic work on Saharan archaeology, *Scavi Sahariani*.[1]

As we have seen, there is evidence that long before the Garamantes arrived in this valley, prehistoric man occupied the cliffs on which rock-artists depicted tropical and even aquatic animals long since vanished from this arid land. There is evidence, too, of a populous and prosperous period shown by the tens of thousands of burial mounds which litter the sides of the bare cliffs; and, even more mysterious, the immense network of underground tunnels running from the base of the cliffs across the valley floor to the oases which lie along the southern limits of the immense sand sea called the Ramla el Dawada. You first become aware of these tunnels, called *foggaras*, as you approach Germa, when the track resembles a switchback railway. Below you is a maze of hundreds of miles of galleries which were presumably built by the Garamantes, though since no careful study has been made of these underground aqueducts, nobody knows for certain when they were constructed or by whom. You can walk along some of them for quite a distance, and you will see that they are quite differently constructed from the Persian *qanats* which are deeper and narrower and provided with a manhole every few hundred yards. The main *foggaras* are sometimes as big as an underground railway tunnel. Many are connected laterally, and the whole system must have supplied an abundance of water sufficient to irrigate thousands of acres of desert soil. Yet it is not proven that these *foggaras* were of Garamantian origin and they could, for that matter, have been constructed by the herdsmen who occupied the Valley before the arrival of the Garamantes; or by some negro race which evidently conquered the area in the Middle Ages. But the Garamantes must be considered the likeliest tunnellers, since such an

1. *Monumenti Antichi*, vol XLI (1951), Rome: Reale Società Geografica Italiana.

enormous undertaking presupposes first, a settled community over a long period of time; and secondly, a huge workforce of slaves. And what does Herodotus say in this connection? 'The Garamantes chase the cave-dwelling Aethiopians in four-horse chariots, for the Aethiopian troglodytes are fleeter of foot than any men we have heard of.' The object of the chase was, of course, to capture slaves for public works which were particularly laborious or hazardous; and such raids actually continued in this region of Africa right into this century. Herodotus's cave-dwelling Aethiopians became a tribe known as the Tibu who still inhabit the mountains of the Tibesti, and for centuries both the Arabs and the Tuareg have harassed these people and used them as serfs in the salt-mines and the palmeries of the desert.

More easily datable than the *foggaras* are the ruins of Roman-type villas and cemeteries which yield up great quantities of Roman artefacts. These villas and burial grounds were suburbs of Garama which we approach through the marshy outskirts of an abandoned oasis. The scene is typical of many such palmeries throughout the Sahara where the old way of life has been virtually destroyed within the last twenty years, though Dr Oudney had noted the already dilapidated state of many of the houses and the impoverishment of the natives when he passed through Germa in 1822. In his day it was, of course, the endemic diseases like malaria, cholera, and dysentery which depopulated the oases. In our times, decline is due to the cessation of the caravan trade and the destruction of the camel-line economy on which the whole region was once dependent. Diesel lorries are replacing the camels; camel-people like the nomadic Tuareg are now considered by the city-based politicians as too independent to fit into schemes for indus-trialization, urbanization, and westernization. The ruins of Germa and many an oasis along the old caravan routes are examples of what has happened in the Sahara.

Germa, then, presents a very desolate scene indeed what with its drooping palms, crumbling houses, and encompassing swamps. The old Turkish citadel, a ruin of jerry-built and brick walls, doesn't add to the gaiety of the place either, especially when one recalls what the early explorers said of the Turkish rule in these parts. But the few archaeologists who have had a chance to excavate at Germa, first the Italians during their occupation and later a small British expedition,[1] found what they had suspected in view of the Roman mausoleum – namely, the foundations of houses which must have been constructed with the aid of skilled quarrymen and masons who knew how to hew and square off blocks of stone. Wherever such buildings dating from the first centuries of our era are found, whether in Europe or Africa, archaeologists are certain that Roman architects and builders have had a hand in their erection. This is not to say that Garama was a Roman city like the great coastal cities of Lepcis Magna and Sabratha, but it undoubtedly indicates that the town was within the imperial sphere of influence and was regularly visited by various military and trade delegations. And it is this fact which explains why the mausoleum stands not far away outside the precincts of the Garamantian capital. Some Roman of importance must have died while on duty here and since the tomb is such an excellent example of funereal architecture, the most likely candidate for such an honour might well have been either the commander of a military force or one of the imperial delegates. We are reminded of Virgil's eulogy of Augustus Caesar – 'This is the man who shall extend his rule beyond the Garamantes . . .' We note the word *beyond*, since the implication is that this African nation was firmly allied with Rome by the time of Augustus.

1. See Charles Daniels, *The Garamantes of Southern Libya*, London: The Oleander Press, 1970.

Who, then, were these Garamantes whose capital was familiar to Romans who had never heard of Londinium of the Britons?

In the total absence of inscriptions, almost all we knew of them before the discovery of their capital city and other monuments along the Wadi el Ajal came from an occasional reference to them in classical authors. The comments of Pliny and Herodotus have already been mentioned. One can add another statement made by the Greek historian that: 'The oxen of the Garamantes move backwards as they graze. The reason is that their horns curve forwards, thus preventing them from going forwards while they graze.' Another author, Pomponius Mela who wrote a geographical account of the inhabited world around AD 40, informs us that: 'the Garamantes do not practise marriage, but live with their women promiscuously, so that children do not know their parents, or parents their children.' Classical authors, we should note, were always scornful of the morals of alien peoples, and the Africans in particular came in for some contemptuous remarks. On the other hand, African societies have always been polygamous and this to a sober-minded Roman like Pomponius Mela was the equivalent of being promiscuous. Julius Caesar seems to have thought the same way about the Britons, for he states rather scornfully that they had ten to twelve wives each, which they shared amongst each other.

But we can now learn much more about these mysterious Garamantes from actual excavations, particularly of their tombs which litter the cliff-sides along the Wadi el Ajal for miles. And out in the open desert a few miles to the west of Germa, a necropolis of some sixty mud-brick pyramids marks the burial ground of the Garamantian kings. In those of the tombs which had not been looted, the Italian archaeologists found Roman dishes, Alexandrian glass, and goblets of native manufacture – the standard 'furniture' of their burial chambers. At the entrance of these tombs stood altars in the form of horns or obelisks, the former representing religious symbols borrowed from the Egyptians and their sun-god Horus; the latter from the Carthaginians and their cult of Tanit. The characteristic offering-tables on which were placed the food and drink needed by the dead man on his journey to the next world were just outside the tombs where relatives could replenish them as necessary.

With the aid of these artefacts, we are able to reconstruct at least some aspects of the religion of the Garamantes. They obviously believed in an after-life since they were interred with the articles they had needed in this world and would presumably require in the next: the tomb furniture usually included useful household utensils like dishes, cups, wine and oil jars, and lamps. Women were buried with a few of their choice ornaments, all this suggesting that their heaven was a continuation of their earthly life, a life, we may be sure, dominated by both awe and fear of natural phenomena, which is the basis of all forms of paganism.

We know that Christian evangelists finally reached this remote country sometime after Christianity had become the official religion of the Empire under Constantine, but we ought not to place too much emphasis on the report of a Byzantine historian that in the year 569 the king of the Garamantes, having concluded a peace treaty with Byzantium, encouraged his subjects to be converted to Christianity, for excavations in and around Germa have so far revealed not a single Christian artefact, let alone the foundations of a Christian church such as we find throughout North Africa where over 2,000 Christian communities and hundreds of Christian buildings have been identified. Clearly the Garamantian king had no success in converting his subjects, though one can assume that his courtiers found it expedient to accept what may have become the official state religion. But a religion imposed by authority from above is one thing; the actual beliefs held by a rustic people is another. It is reasonable to suppose that the Garamantes went on worshipping – or placating, rather – their pagan gods, as many Africans continue to do to-day, despite the claims of Christian missionaries.

But whereas we can make an educated guess at the nature of the Garamantian religion, we still know next to nothing of the customs, economy, and social structure of a nation which appears in history as far back as the fifth century BC and disappears 1,000 years later when Okba ibn-Nafi, the Arab commander, conquered the Fezzan in AD 663. His biographer Ibn-Khaldoun tells a strange story of this event.

Having cut off the ear of the king of Waddan and exacted a tribute of 360 slaves, Okba desired to know what kind of country lay beyond Waddan. They told him of Germa, capital of the whole Fezzan. Leaving Waddan, he arrived after a march of eight nights on the outskirts of Germa whose inhabitants he invited to embrace Islam. They agreed, and he called a halt six miles from the town.

When the king of the Garamantes came out from Germa to meet Okba, the Arab horsemen rode in between the king and his escort, forcing them to dismount and to walk on foot the six miles to where Okba was camped. Since the king was sickly, he arrived in an exhausted state, spitting blood.

'Why do you treat me like this after I have yielded to you?' the Garamantian king asked.

'It will teach you a lesson not to make war on the Arabs,' Okba replied as was his custom. And he sent the king back to Egypt in chains.[1]

---

1. Abd al-Rahman ibn Muhammad, called ibn Khaldun, *Histoires des Berbères*, traduite par M. le baron de Slane, Vol I, p 196, Alger: Imprimerie du Gouvernement, 1852–6.

The Garamantes, had existed as an independent nation for at least 1,000 years during which time they controlled one of the most ancient and important of the caravan routes coming up from Central Africa. The trans-Saharan trade, in fact, was important enough for the Romans to have sent two expeditions as far as Garama, that of Cornelius Balbus in 20 BC and a second led by Julius Maternus in about AD 100. The Romans were undoubtedly interested in reconnoitring as well as protecting the caravan routes; hence there is a possibility that Julius Maternus, who was accompanied by the king of the Garamantes, may during a campaign which lasted four months have marched as far south as the Niger River – 'to a country inhabited by negroes, called Agisymba, where the rhinoceros congregate', according to the Greek geographer Ptolemy writing in the middle of the second century of the Christian era.

What, then, were the products of Central Africa which were conveyed through the territories of the Garamantes and were so important to Rome? Undoubtedly the most prized was ivory, used not only for making images of the gods, but also for the manufacture of many luxury articles. In fact, so much ivory was consumed in the Greek, Alexandrian, and Roman workshops that the elephants which once roamed north of the Atlas Mountains had been wiped out by the end of the Republic. Additional supplies were now brought up from Central Africa – 'beyond the Syrtic deserts', as Pliny tells us in a reference to the trans-Saharan caravan trade. The caravans also carried the much-prized ostrich feathers and a quantity of gold dust produced in the mines of West Africa whose whereabouts remained a mystery to Europeans almost to the end of the nineteenth century. But the most valuable of all the African exports consisted of exotic wild beasts destined to be slaughtered by their thousands in the Roman arenas.

Some idea of the number and variety of wild beasts used in the games at Rome alone is seen from the statistics given by

Roman historians. In 55 BC Pompey celebrated his victories by turning loose 600 lions in the arena during the five days devoted to the *venatio*: that is, simulated hunting in the amphitheatre. In AD 81 the emperor Titus contributed 9,000 animals for the spectacle; twenty-five years later, Trajan raised this total to 11,000. In AD 248 the emperor Philip, an Arab by birth and (according to Gibbon) 'consequently, in the earlier part of his life, a robber by profession', solemnized the secular games by killing in the arena 32 elephants, 10 eland, 10 tigers, 70 lions, 30 leopards, 10 hyenas, one rhinoceros, one hippopotamus, 10 giraffes, 20 zebras, and 10 wild horses. We also read that the emperor Probus in one day in AD 281 sacrificed 1,000 ostriches, 1,000 stags, 1,000 fallow-deer, and 1,000 wild boars; while on the following day 100 lions, 100 lionesses, 200 leopards, and 300 bears were slaughtered in the arena. Literally thousands of these animals must have been brought from Central Africa; and if we add to this total the thousands of others which were supplied to amphitheatres all over the Roman world, we can see why an obscure nation like the Garamantes, who may have trapped as well as transported these wild creatures, grew rich in the process. For the cages containing lions, giraffes, ostriches, zebras, hippopotami, and even rhinoceroses were carted across the desert, and nearly all of this traffic seems to have passed through their territory. This nation, then, like those nations of Arabia which lay along the old Incense Road, prospered greatly from the intercontinental trade, for there can be no other explanation of how this remote African kingdom could afford the sophisticated Roman houses and villas found in and around Germa and the quantity of imported goods, both household and luxury articles, unearthed by the archaeologists.[1]

1. See Ayoub, M.S., *Excavations at Germa, the Capital of the Garamantes, 1962–1966*, Tripoli: Government Printing Office, 1967.

There are also other indications of the former prosperity of this whole region of the Fezzan. The escarpments of the cliffs which border the Wadi el Ajal on the south are covered with tens of thousands of rock tombs or burial mounds. Nobody has yet counted the number of these graves, but it is estimated that there are at least 100,000 of them. This bespeaks a large resident population, and, as we have seen, the extent of the irrigation system proves the importance of agriculture in the Valley. We know that North Africa was always regarded as the granary of Rome, and we also know that the problems of feeding the enormous population of the metropolis became more acute as the empire expanded. The authorities were always looking for new sources of supply; and while it is difficult to see how grain, for instance, could have been exported in bulk from the Fezzan, it is quite certain that certain specific locally produced products had to pay for imports. But what precisely these local products consisted of has puzzled historians since the discovery of Garama. Some commentators have suggested gold which was always in short supply in the Roman empire as the entire imports from the East – incense, spices, rare woods, silk, and so forth – had to be paid for in bullion. The Garamantes mined no gold themselves, of course, but they could have been the caravaners who brought it across the desert from the West African mines, as later the Arabs were to do throughout the Middle Ages. Other commentators suggest the special trade was in slaves, and certainly slave-trading enriched the Fezzan enormously from the sixth to the twentieth century. But the Romans had all the slaves they needed from their conquests in Europe and the Near East; and they had no particular use for black slaves as the plantation owners of the West Indies and the Americas were to have in later years. But all such suggestions are speculative, and until further excavations are undertaken, we are bound to admit that on the evidence available all we can say is that the Garamantes were a populous and prosperous people and the Fezzan (the Phazania of the classical geographers) was a fertile region loosely allied to Rome by military, political, and commercial ties.

It is this evidence which makes the wretched mosquito-ridden village of Germa such a grim reminder of the rise and fall of nations. Along the whole Valley, so rich in monuments and memories, only a few hundred people eke out a sparse existence in the string of oases, of which Germa is only one. They no longer have any significant communication with the outside world – certainly nothing like their predecessors had. The Fezzan produces scarcely any commodities worth exporting and can no longer grow rich on the trans-Saharan trade.

And so the Garamantes and their capital Germa have disappeared almost completely from historical memory and survive to-day, as far as they survive at all, only as a footnote in the textbooks on Roman Africa. We do not even know for certain who they were, where they came from, or what became of them after the Arab conquest of AD 663 and the exile of their last king. Here again speculation comes into its own. As for their origin, the assumption is that they came from Asia Minor. It is a theory based on Herodotus's statement that they chased their negro neighbours in four-horse chariots. The chariot was undoubtedly an importation from Asia Minor. Neither the horse nor the cart was known in pre-classical Africa outside of Egypt. Where, then, did the Garamantes obtain their horses and chariots? We can guess that they brought them with them when they invaded the Fezzan. They would also have brought their own language, customs, and weapons.

If, then, the Garamantes belonged to the Caucasian race, were they the ancestors of the Tuareg, the 'Veiled Men' who took over their empire and exercised control of the trans-Saharan caravan trade which had so enriched the ancient nation of the Fezzan? This fascinating theory, first proposed by the

Italian anthropologist Sergio Sergi, is partly based on the fact that the Tuareg are so strikingly different in physique, manners, and language from other desert people. They are certainly taller than the Berbers or Arabs or hybrid descendants of Arab masters and negro slaves. Their men are veiled, their women not. Their spoken and written language have their roots in Old Libyan and Punic, not Arabic. And finally, though they are Moslems, they seem to have inherited from somebody – and certainly not from the Arab conquerors of the Fezzan – certain Christian words and symbols which again makes them unique among the Moslems of Africa.

But here, as in almost everything to do with this 'lost' nation of ancient history, we are in the realms of speculation, and it is now too late to learn anything from the Tuareg. A hundred years ago this might have been possible, for at that time this unusual people was flourishing. But tribal life is changing so rapidly in Africa that it will soon be impossible to discover their origins. Already the younger generation have only a smattering of their spoken language called Temajegh, and very few indeed can write the script called T'ifinagh which used to record their deeds as well as their poems and songs. The Tuareg warrior of the last century, a tall man in his black veil, perched aloft a white racing camel, and armed with *les armes blanches* – spear and leather shield – is a figure of the past, along with his possible ancestor, the Garamantian in his chariot, or, for that matter, the Roman centurion who may lie buried in the mausoleum just outside the 'renowned city' of Garama.

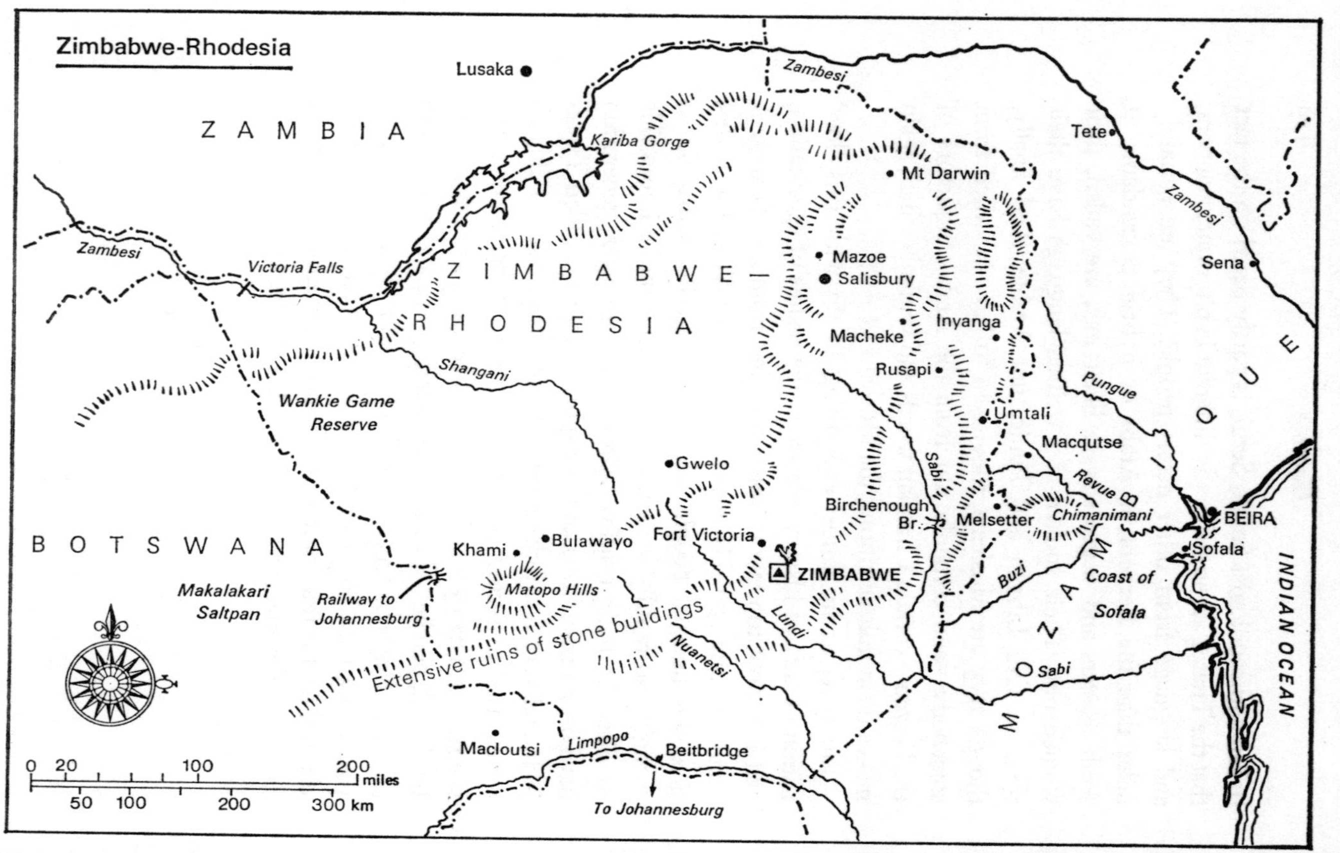

Zimbabwe-Rhodesia
ZAMBIA
Lusaka
Zambesi
Kariba Gorge
Tete
Mt Darwin
Zambesi
Zambesi
Victoria Falls
ZIMBABWE—
Mazoe
Salisbury
Sena
RHODESIA
Macheke
Inyanga
Rusapi
Shangani
Pungue
Wankie Game
Reserve
Umtali
Macqutse
Revue
Gwelo
Sabi
Birchenough
Br.
Melsetter
Chimanimani
BEIRA
BOTSWANA
Khami
Bulawayo
Fort Victoria
ZIMBABWE
Buzi
Coast of
Sofala
Sofala
INDIAN OCEAN
Makalakari
Saltpan
Railway to
Johannesburg
Matopo Hills
Lundi
Extensive ruins of stone buildings
Nuanetsi
Sabi
Macloutsi
Limpopo
Beitbridge
0   20   100   200
                            miles
50   100   200   300 km
To Johannesburg

Zimbabwe

Everything about the lost city of Zimbabwe is strange, and the significance of this pile of stones transcends by far the historical and archaeological facts and leads the investigator into the most curious bypaths of socio-political speculation. For, as we shall see, all the controversies, indeed the animosities, arising from the racial issue are implicit in the story of Zimbabwe and its origin.

That story begins with the hint of mystery with which it ends, for we are not even sure who discovered the site and notified the world of its existence. Certainly the Arabs visited it in the course of their trading missions which took them over almost the whole of Africa long before the Europeans had done more than establish a hold on the northern and western coasts. But the Arab traders were not interested in ruins, and even their great scholar-travellers like Ibn Battuta who visited the East African coast around 1325 were somewhat indifferent to lost or abandoned cities of pre-Islamic times. As for the Portuguese who occupied and colonized the East African coast from the beginning of the sixteenth to the end of the nineteenth century, they never really penetrated very far inland into the country vaguely known as Monomotapa, an actual kingdom according to some, a legendary realm according to others. But too much scepticism is unjustified in view of the unanimous opinion of the Portuguese writers that there was such a country ruled over by a powerful chieftain called Mutota. This chieftain had conquered sometime in the mid-fifteenth century a huge area of south-east Africa bounded by the Indian Ocean, the Limpopo and Zambesi rivers, and the Kalahari Desert. Some idea of his character and methods can be seen from his honorific title, *Mwene Mutapa*, meaning 'master-pillager'. *Mwene Mutapa* is Bantu and became transliterated into Monomotapa: that is, the kingdom of Mutota, the heartland of which was Rhodesia, capital Zimbabwe.

So much we learn from the Portuguese chroniclers, but understandably a great deal of what they record is hearsay, based on information or rumour brought back from the hinterland by the Arab traders. The Portuguese themselves were chary about moving too far from the coast, for the obvious reasons that the climate was unsuitable for European colonists, the country was mosquito- and tsetse fly-ridden, and communications with the base-camps difficult to maintain. So the Portuguese were never as close as the Arabs to the tribes, and their knowledge of the natives, in consequence, was negligible until the arrival of the Jesuit missionaries in 1560. These brave and dedicated priests did penetrate Monomotapa, did live with the Africans, and did convert the tribal chiefs whom they described as 'showing a great facility in receiving the faith' – a rather optimistic claim in view of the alacrity with which the new converts later rejected it.

The speculation over Zimbabwe can really be reduced in its simplest form to 'Who built this place – white or black men'? Judging from the degree of technical skill of the present bush-Africans, is it conceivable that such large and relatively sophisticated constructions could have been designed and built by their ancestors? Implied in these leading questions is the once unquestioned belief that negroes could not possibly have erected the elaborate constructions found at Zimbabwe since they never evolved beyond the Iron Age and, in fact, were in most respects still in the neolithic stage; they never invented a system of writing; they had no knowledge of mathematics, let alone geometry; and they had never discovered how to dress and build in stone. The German explorer, Dr Heinrich Schlichter, stated the conclusion with Teutonic finality:

> It was clear from the outset that the buildings could not possibly have been erected by African savages.[1]

Accepting this premise as incontrovertible, all the early excavators and students of the Rhodesian site propounded the most extraordinary and bizarre theories to explain the origin of these, the most evocative ruins in Africa. It is easy now for complacent career-archaeologists of the modern variety to scoff at these first explorers; but at least we can admit that these pioneers brought enormous enthusiasm as well as interest to the search for the ultimate truth of Zimbabwe. And as partial compensation for the absurdity of some of their theories – not to mention the damage they did to the archaeological evidence! – we have their vivid descriptions of an Africa before that wonderfully endowed continent with all its interesting peoples and animals was, as it continues to be, ruined by its despoilers.

The Portuguese, who were the first to hear of a large stone city somewhere in the kingdom of Monomotapa, were not, of course, looking for historical monuments, but for the gold which was thought to be so abundant in these newly discovered territories. The Jesuit priests, for their part, were after the souls of the natives, and they had neither the time nor the inclination to collect information about the people, their history, customs, and social organization, especially as the occasional murder of their missionaries forced them to abandon stations too far from their headquarters in Sofala. At the same

1. Henry Schlichter, 'The Ruins of Mashonaland', *The Geographical Journal*, February, 1893, p 2.

time, scholars back in Europe, hearing of the new African Eldorado and associating it with the Biblical references to Ophir, the port from whence Phoenician ships brought back gold for Solomon's temple, actually began to ask whether Monomotapa might not be the land of King Solomon's Mines.

Ophir, according to the Book of Kings, was the destination of the Tarshish ships which after a three-year voyage returned with gold, silver, precious stones, costly woods, ivory, apes, and peacocks. All of these articles with the exception of peacocks (and for this animal some Hebrew scholars read ostriches) were to be found in East Africa, particularly the first of these products, the famous 'gold of Ophir'. Further evidence was adduced from Herodotus's account of the circumnavigation of Africa by Phoenician ships, since it was the vessels of this great maritime nation which Solomon had commissioned to bring back the precious cargoes. Before long, reports were coming in of traces of Phoenician pottery and of mining operations in the vicinity of Zimbabwe; and, even more convincing, statements by German travellers that the Arabs had always regarded the stone city as the Ophir of Solomon. All these bits and pieces of information seemed to tally with the early reports by the Portuguese captains concerning the wealth of the fallen kingdom of Monomotapa, whose gold mines were said to yield several hundred thousand pounds of metal a year.

Rumours of great and splendid cities in the interior of Africa had begun circulating in Europe with the publication of an annual report, a sort of 'Blue Book' entitled *Da Asia*, compiled by the Portuguese civil servant João de Barros and issued from 1552 to 1613. It is in this book that we get the first hint of Zimbabwe, or the description of a stone fortress-city which sounds very much like it, 'with a tower more than twelve fathoms [72 feet] high'. Unfortunately de Barros was reporting the sort of exaggerated gossip that circulated in the souks of

Sofala, the small Arab settlement in Mozambique, captured by the Portuguese in 1505 and made the headquarters of their Captaincy of south-east Africa. Such gossip was, and still is, typical of the traveller's tales which come out of Africa, so that we need not be astonished to hear of an African chieftain's palace described by an eighteenth-century traveller as having 'sumptuous apartments, spacious and lofty halls, floors, ceilings, beams, and rafters plated with gold . . . plates, dishes, and bowls belonging to the Emperor's table made of a sort of porcelain . . . In short so rich and magnificent is this palace that it may be said to vie with that which distinguishes a monarch of the East.'[1] With descriptions like this it is no wonder that when Zimbabwe was finally discovered by an American in 1868 all the myths and fantasies based on the legend of King Solomon's Mines should reassert themselves, with the result that Monomotapa, the land we now call Zimbabwe-Rhodesia,[2] was to experience a gold-rush comparable with that of Alaska.

But despite the number of hunters, prospectors, archaeologists, and travel-writers who were wandering about this unexplored country in the latter half of the last century, the mystery of Zimbabwe remained, enveloping in a sense all those who went in search of it, in particular that mythical American who actually discovered it but, alas! left scarcely any trace of himself or of his life as an exile in Black Africa of the 1860s, for what a story he could have told. Our principal reference to Adam Renders (or Render) comes from a Mr E. A. Maund, a British political agent whose assignment was to bring two old headmen (their ages were sixty-five and seventy) of King Lobengula of Mashonaland back to England

1. George Henry Millar, *The New and Universal System of Geography*, London: printed for A. Hogg, 1783, p 339.
2. As of 1979.

and to present them to Queen Victoria in 1888. Reporting on his experiences to the Royal Geographical Society, Mr Maund states that: 'a man named Renders who was living on the top of a kopje [the South African word for 'a small hill'] a few miles south-west of Zimbabwe, was really the first to discover the ruins, three years before Herr Mauch saw them, though Mauch and Baines first published them to the world.'[1]

We learn a little more of Renders from this same Herr Mauch, a German geologist who was the first to describe in print the wonders of Zimbabwe and who was in consequence credited with being their discoverer, though he does tell us how he was taken to see the ruins by Adam Render (as he calls him), a professional hunter who had come from the Transvaal and settled down with a black woman. It appears that Mauch had been ambushed, robbed, and abandoned in the bush where Renders rescued him. And that is the last we hear of this mysterious American who is said to have died and to have been buried near the ruins he discovered.

The German Karl G. Mauch was, however, the man who put Zimbabwe on the map, although he generously gave Adam Renders credit for being the first white man to have seen the fabled stone city. But Renders was manifestly not the type to be particularly interested in ruins: he was more concerned with the everyday business of survival. Mauch, on the other hand, was a typical product of his time and his country, well educated, intelligent, adventurous, and enterprising. And like so many of the great explorers of his century – and the Germans were amongst the most illustrious of them – he travelled alone. He was alone and actually lost somewhere near the Tokwe River when he was robbed of everything he had and, as he tells us, had given up hope of surviving. But immediately

---

1. *Proceedings of the Royal Geographical Society*, Vol XIII, February, 1891, pp 105, 106.

after Renders had succoured him, he continued his careful and detailed study of the great ruins.

Karl Mauch, then, as a serious explorer, was deeply interested in ancient history and capable of appreciating the uniqueness of what to Renders and an Englishman named George Phillips who also saw the ruins in 1868 was just another pile of stones. Mauch even shouted 'Bravo!' when he first saw the great walls from five miles away.

> It was the very place for which I had been searching since 1868. What wonderful luck and how utterly unexpected! For days on end I had been in hourly dread of death and now I was standing on the threshold of my greatest achievement. Heaven be praised![1]

His survey of Zimbabwe certainly was a great achievement, for he had to work under the most difficult conditions on account of the hostility of the local tribesmen who at first would not let him visit the city at all. These Africans behaved exactly like the Arabs who harassed Burckhardt at Petra, and hence it was a superb accomplishment on the part of both the Swiss and the German to survey, measure, and make plans of their discoveries. At first Mauch had to visit the ruins at night; and since he had been robbed of all his surveying equipment, he had to make his calculations by eye or by a home-made yard-stick of some sort. Consequently some of his measurements are a long way out, though not that of the famous conical tower up which he climbed by means of a creeper and which he estimated, correctly, to be thirty feet high, eight feet in diameter at the top, and solidly built. Only a travel-toughened man of thirty-four could have accomplished such a feat as

1. Karl G. Mauch, 'Reisen im Inneren von Süd Afrika, 1865–72', *Petermanns Geographische Mitteilungen* (1874), p 37; published in translation in *Native Affairs Department (Rhodesia) Annual*, 1952, No 29.

surveying a site covered with impenetrable foliage which actually concealed many of the buildings. And as so often happened throughout this great period of African exploration, the explorer paid dearly for his zeal. He had contracted cerebral malaria during his wanderings, and four years after his homecoming to Germany, he fell out of a window during a fit brought on by a prolonged fever and died aged only thirty-eight.

Mauch was, of course, primarily a geologist rather than an historian, and his mistake was to propound a fanciful and, indeed, foolish theory which not only brought ridicule on himself, but engendered a certain scepticism among scholars as to the genuineness of his discovery. In brief, the German declared that the fortress he had seen and examined on the top of the hill (the ruin now known as 'The Acropolis') was a copy of King Solomon's Temple in Jerusalem, while the Valley Ruins, as they are now called, were a copy of the palace the Queen of Sheba occupied during her visit to the Jewish monarch. Evidently Mauch's theory was founded on the myth that Zimbabwe was the ruin of an Israelite colony identical with the Ophir of the Old Testament. While such a pronouncement inevitably excited the scorn of professional historians, it delighted the cranks and inspired the novelists. The theme of Rider Haggard's *King Solomon's Mines*, first published in 1885 and a world-wide best-seller for the next fifty years, was derived from the unusual public interest in Zimbabwe resulting from Karl Mauch's revelations.

Mauch's theory, even more than the discovery itself, was highly significant on two counts: first, it romanticized the African ruins; and secondly, it set the fashion for all subsequent theories of the 'white' origin of Zimbabwe. The German traveller's identification of the ruins with King Solomon, in short, was based on the assumption that black men could never have built the 'Temple' and 'Acropolis' of this Rhodesian city,

The Maya had dozens of obscure gods, and their abandoned city of Copán is only one of many mysteries surrounding their forgotten culture. Frederick Catherwood, artist on the expedition which discovered Copán, drew exquisite pictures of their religious monuments

Raleigh's first colonizing expedition to Virginia arrived off Roanoke Island in 1585. This engraving was made from a watercolour drawing by John White, Governor of the lost City of Raleigh

since they had never built anything comparable anywhere else in Africa. Hence men of a white or Caucasian race must have come from somewhere to have erected the Zimbabwe monuments or to have shown the natives how to work with stone.

One consequence of this premise was that the next explorers of Zimbabwe, Theodore and Mabel Bent, the delightful husband-and-wife team who subsequently explored the coast of South Arabia, were enticed, as it were, into putting forward still another absurd theory. The great elliptical structure of the 'Temple' which had caused Mauch to shout 'Bravo! That's it!' when he first saw the huge stone wall on that September day of 1871 was bound to incite in an amateur and romantically disposed archaeologist like Theodore Bent that characteristic Victorian fondness for prehistoric 'temples' associated with astronomical calculations, Stonehenge being the favourite example (as, for that matter, it still is). Spurred on by his surveyor Robert Swan, Bent was easily convinced that the Zimbabwe 'Temple' was erected by the same race of men who built the Temple of Ilumquh, the moon-god, at Marib in the Yemen. So now Mauch's *Israelites* became Bent's *Sabaeans*, a people best known to us from the Biblical reference to the Land of Sheba and its mythological queen.[1]

But even if Theodore Bent, like Karl Mauch, belonged to that school of traveller-antiquarians whose theories are nowadays as outmoded as the manner in which they travelled, they nevertheless wrote the most entertaining of books, books which can never be written again, for these explorers were seeing Africa in its primeval condition.[2] Theodore and his wife Mabel ('the only one of our party who escaped fever, never having a day's sickness during the whole year we were

1. See Chapter 2.
2. James Theodore Bent, *The Ruined Cities of Mashonaland*, Longmans: London, 1892.

away'), accompanied by the cartographer Robert Swan, set out from Kimberley in South Africa with two wagons, thirty-six oxen, and heaps of tinned provisions, stopping *en route* to study the customs of the various people through whose territory they passed. Theodore had the curiosity as well as the open mind of his great contemporary Richard Burton, and was mercifully never coy about what he had to report to the end of adding to the sum of knowledge, whether it was the total nudity of the natives or the decorations across the bellies of the women in the form of rows of cicatrices which he attempted to count, reaching the total of sixteen 'when the bashful female ran away'. Calamities, like curiosities, had to be accepted by the old African travellers with equanimity. At Fort Victoria, which then as now was the jumping-off place for Zimbabwe some seventeen miles away, Theodore found every single resident down with fever and 150 saddles placed in rows within the fort representing the 150 horses brought in by the settlers. Every horse had died of the mysterious 'horse sickness', the only known cure for which was to dose the animal with a bottle of whisky, a medicine successfully administered in the case of one of the Bents' three horses.

It took Theodore and Mabel seven days' march from Fort Victoria to the Ruins, ferrying their ox-wagons across crocodile-infested streams with the help of the native hunters who spent most of their time shooting mice ('a great delicacy beloved by them') and collecting bagfuls of hairy brown caterpillars to supplement their rations. Eventually camp was set up at Zimbabwe on 6 June 1891 and the first investigation of the Ruins began.

We have already mentioned that Theodore Bent was not an archaeologist in the modern sense, but what used to be termed an *antiquarian*. His colleague, Robert Swan, on the other hand, was one of those eccentrics who had become completely obsessed with the cosmological method of dating ancient ruins.

The assumption underlying this method is that all prehistoric people built their monuments according to specific astronomical phenomena. Swan assumed, for instance, that the so-called 'Temple of Zimbabwe' was a religious structure, whence he easily convinced himself and half-convinced his colleague that it was a giant observatory for ascertaining the time of the summer solstice. At first accepting the theoretical assumptions as well as the actual measurements of the surveyor as conclusive (and both were later to be proved wrong), Theodore later jumped to other false conclusions, involving himself in more and more outlandish speculations. He asserts that the famous conical tower inside the 'Temple' or 'great Enclosure' corresponded to all those penis-like structures mentioned by classical authors, thus proving that the African ruins were contemporaneous with the ancient civilizations. It is true, of course, that phallus-like stones, some of which are still *in situ*, are positioned along the top of the 'Temple' wall, so that the possibility of some cult connected with these symbols must be taken into account; but a great deal of scientific mumbo-jumbo seems to have resulted from Bent's observations, reaching its apogee of absurdity in the conclusion of R. N. Hall, a freelance journalist of antiquarian inclinations who was made Curator of the Ruins in 1902:

> We can imagine that here [in the Temple] was the college and its professors of the complicated ritual and deep learning which research has shown to have been the characteristics of the Phallic worship, for the people [i.e., the residents of Zimbabwe], who were educated in scientific matters to an extent almost beyond modern conception, would not be ruled over by an uneducated priesthood.[1]

1. R. N. Hall and W. G. Neal, *The Ancient Ruins of Rhodesia*, 2nd ed, London: Methuen, 1904, p 199.

One is inclined to ask if Mr Hall is not pulling our leg, except that he continually returns to this theory in his subsequent writings and lectures, though he nowhere proves that 'deep learning' is necessary to understand what 'Phallic worship' is all about.

Theodore Bent who spent six months clearing, surveying, and examining the ruins, made the most dramatic find of all – the eight famous birds carved in soapstone and placed atop five-foot pillars sited in and around the great elliptical 'Temple'. He considered them to be hawks or vultures. Subsequent archaeologists have identified the birds as hornbills, African fish eagles, and so forth. Whatever the species of the fowls, all agree that they had some ritualistic function, perhaps featuring in some form of ancestor rites, or rain-making ceremonies. Bent noted that the pedestals were phallic-shaped carvings whose 'anatomical accuracy unmistakably proves that circumcision was practised by this primitive race'. Circumcision, of course fitted in nicely with his Sabaean thesis, since these early Arabs were thought to practise the rite along with their Semitic cousins, the Israelites.

Bent's other finds included fragments of decorated bowls in soapstone; a few pieces of Chinese pottery, Persian ware, and Arabian glass; and a variety of bronze and iron weapons.[1] All of these artefacts quickly led him to postulate a connection with the ancient world. He starts out with a 'Phoenician theory' on the grounds that a soapstone mould he unearthed resembled the ingot of tin found in Falmouth Harbour (and associated with the Phoenician tin trade between the Mediterranean and Cornwall). 'This is very presumptive evidence,' he writes, 'that the gold workers of ancient Zimbabwe worked for the Phoenician market.' But despite the 'very presumptive evidence', he finally opts for the South Arabians on the sup-

1. Bent, *op cit*, Ch VI.

position that the Temple of Ilumquh at Marib and the 'Temple' of Zimbabwe are the work of one and the same people.

> The points of comparison are so very strong, and there is furthermore a strong connection between the star-worshipping Sabaeans and the temple with its points orientated to the sun and built on such definite mathematical principles.[1]

Bent's surveyor Swan was, of course, responsible for this nonsense about 'mathematical principles', which he attempts to explain in the Appendix to *The Ruined Cities of Mashonaland*. But however conscientiously one tries to understand what this Scotsman is talking about, one ends by being completely baffled by his pseudo-science.

With the publication of Theodore Bent's and Richard Hall's extremely readable books in 1892 and 1902 respectively, the British public became more and more interested in Zimbabwe. The Matabele Wars of the 1890s, now as remote to us as the Punic Wars of the third century BC, had been front-page news, and the name of Lobengula, King of the Matabele, as familiar to newspaper readers as the more notorious African presidents of to-day. The Matabeles, King Lobengula, the gold-mines of Mashonaland, and the Ruins of Zimbabwe were all news and all the subjects of reports from 'Our Special Correspondent'. The excitement was intense. Theodore Bent's books went through three editions in three years, and amazement over his finds increased still further when the German traveller Dr Heinrich Schlichter announced that he had been able to date the 'Citadel' to 1100 BC. Since no layman in those days had the temerity to question a German savant, King Solomon and the Queen of Sheba were again the favourites for the distinction of having built Zimbabwe.

Some nine years after the publication of Theodore Bent's

1. Bent, *op cit*, p ix.

sensational *The Ruined Cities of Mashonaland* appeared *The Ancient Ruins of Rhodesia*[1] by Richard Hall, a freelance journalist, and William Neal, a gold-miner – a seemingly odd pair to be dabbling in archaeology; but what they lacked in academic prestige, they made up for in enthusiasm and hard work, for Hall and Neal dug away for many years at dozens of sites in Southern Rhodesia and give invaluable summaries of stone ruins all over the country. Uninhibited by the fear of the professional archaeologists, unaware of the sophisticated techniques of modern excavators, the co-authors produced an enormous book which, like Bent's *The Ruined Cities*, at once became a best-seller, for by now the Americans as well as the British public were highly intrigued by discussions about Ophir, King Solomon's mines, the Phoenician trade routes, and the Sabaean colonies, not to mention 'Phallic worship' and 'astronomical temples', just as to-day people exhibit the same sort of interest in Bermuda Triangles, Unidentified Flying Objects, and Visitors from Outer Space. Messrs Hall and Neal being wholly free of the doubts which assailed more cautious historians followed what by now had become almost the orthodox line and flatly declared that the Ophir of Scripture was definitely located in the country of Monomotapa of which Zimbabwe was the capital.

It is now obvious that all the dangerous explorations and careful surveys of these African ruins by Theodore Bent, Richard Hall, W. G. Neal, and distinguished European scholar-travellers such as Karl Mauch and Dr Heinrich Schlichter had in a sense been wasted, since their findings in every case had been vitiated by a false premise. Each of these pioneers had simply proved what he erroneously assumed – not one feels, out of conscious racial prejudice, but out of

1. Richard Nicklin Hall and W. G. Neal, *The Ancient Ruins of Rhodesia – Monomotapae Imperium*, Methuen: London, 1902.

respect for official anthropological doctrine: to wit, there was no evidence anywhere in the African continent that the aboriginals, be they Bantu or Bushmen, were capable of erecting the kind of structures found at Zimbabwe. And this was not a slur upon Africans. It was supposed to be a statement of fact; and it was pointless to argue about facts.

But this is exactly what was to happen with the appearance on the scene of the professional archaeologists who were a very different breed from the old-fashioned antiquaries who had been pottering around ruins since the time of William Camden (1551–1623), the prototype of the wandering scholar. The first of the new men, in fact, was typical of the new school and the forerunner of the field archaeologists one finds to-day in charge of expeditions in remote places. This newcomer to Zimbabwe was Dr David Randall-MacIver, a Scotsman who had studied Egyptology at Oxford and then worked with Sir Flinders Petrie in Egypt. His education and training had combined to make him very disdainful of the antiquarians, journalists, treasure-seekers, and gold-miners who had been digging around in the now-famous Ruins for the twenty years before his arrival in 1905. And within a couple of months, this energetic excavator had dug up enough of the site to publish a comprehensive report in which he dismissed the theories of all his predecessors as nonsense.

Randall-MacIver declared on the basis of his excavations that:

1) Zimbabwe was no older than the medieval period;
2) the earliest possible date for its foundation was the fourteenth century AD;
3) the great stone buildings had been designed and erected by Africans.[1]

1. David Randall-MacIver, *Mediaeval Rhodesia*, London: Macmillan 1906.

The controversy that followed was not confined to the experts. While conservative scholars found Randall-MacIver's conclusions too radical, the lay public were not inclined to give up the more romantic theories of Bent and Hall so easily, particularly as the Scotsman assumed a hectoring tone in his criticism of his predecessors. Even admitting that Theodore Bent was an amateur antiquarian and Richard Hall a journalist, was not Randall-MacIver something of a dilettante himself, Egyptologist, Etruscologist, and Iron-Age historian in turn?

But despite all the criticisms of *Mediaeval Rhodesia* and the announcement of new ideas intended to save the 'white' theory of the origin of Zimbabwe – one such being that the 'Acropolis' and 'Temple' had been designed and built by Arabs – Randall-MacIver was unanimously supported by his fellow-archaeologists. There seemed nothing else to say on the subject: all talk of King Solomon, Ophir, and the Sabaeans was silenced by derision, until Zimbabwe once again became news when another excavator belonging to the same rigidly disciplined school as Randall-MacIver began to dig in the Ruins *and came to a different conclusion as to the date of their foundation.* Miss Gertrude Caton-Thompson, aided by two trained women colleagues, re-excavated Zimbabwe in 1929 and declared on the evidence of the Chinese pottery and beads found there by Theodore Bent that the original foundation of the city probably went back to the eighth century AD, thus making it some 600 years older than Randall-MacIver had allowed. Moreover, Miss Thompson disagreed with Randall-MacIver and the other experts on other matters, notably the purpose and significance of the famous Conical Tower. Bent had believed this Tower to have been used as a shrine for 'Phallic worship'. Hall categorized it more simply as 'a huge phallus' (not surprisingly in view of the fact that it is all of thirty-one feet high). The German Dr Heinrich Schlichter had considered it a gnomon 'or measuring device'. Samuel Dornan, the anthropologist, reckoned it was a chieftain's grave. And Randall-MacIver had pronounced it 'the symbol of a chief's power', which was safer than Leo Frobenius's guess of a 'sacrificial ant-hill', whatever that may mean. Miss Caton-Thompson comes to a rather surprising conclusion, going back to the first theory, that of Theodore Bent, and then linking the phallic cult petrified, as it were, in the shape of the Tower with the comparable shape of the primitive Arab minaret. And so the Arabs or some other intruders reappear on the Zimbabwe scene, the resultant controversy being neatly summed up by the Rhodesian anthropologist F. W. T. Posselt:

> On the one hand, it is claimed that they [the Zimbabwe ruins] are evidence of a very early occupation; on the other, that they are of recent – that is, Bantu – origin. It would seem that neither view is without objection, and it might be suggested that they were constructed by means of Bantu labour, but under the direction and control of some other race.[1]

Miss Caton-Thompson, who was far less dogmatic than her immediate predecessor, was prepared to consider this point of view, for while she insists that Zimbabwe was built by Africans, she admits that: 'no one would deny the possibility – rather they would urge the inevitability – of exotic stimuli, physical and cultural, received and absorbed during ages of coastal contact with alien trading peoples. I have even ventured to suggest one or two features in the Zimbabwe buildings which may perhaps not unreasonably be attributed to a foreign original.'[2] And she adds that as far as the actual building technique was concerned, 'this was the product of an infantile

1. F. W. T. Posselt, *A Survey of the Native Tribes of Southern Rhodesia*, Salisbury: Native Affairs Department, 1927, pp 2–3.
2. Gertrude Caton-Thompson, *The Zimbabwe Culture. Ruins and Reactions*, Clarendon Press: Oxford, 1931, pp 2–3.

mind, a mind which having discovered the way of making or doing a thing goes on childishly repeating the performance regardless of incongruity'.[1]

Although surveys and excavations continue to be made at Zimbabwe[2], Miss Caton-Thompson has deservedly had the last word on the subject, for her studies of the Ruins were by far and away the most detailed and revealing of all the digs, even though when she began work at the site in 1929, almost a score of archaeologists, professional and amateur, plus the usual treasure-hunters, had poked about in the area, disturbing vital evidence and completely wrecking certain of the most important complexes. Nevertheless, this English archaeologist has revealed all the material evidence we are now likely to uncover at Zimbabwe, and it only remains for her successors to preserve the site as a splendid monument of a mysterious past.

As for the visitor, assuming he listens to all the theories as to the origins of Zimbabwe and the arguments as to who were the architects, he is quite likely to end his tour as he began it, mystified by what he has seen and, even more, by what he has been told. The controversies certainly continue, and their resolution is not made any easier now that racial prejudices have become more important or, at least, more emotive, than archaeological facts. Thus, those who champion the cause of what the French call *négritude* will go on arguing that the Zimbabwe and other Rhodesian stone monuments are not only the unassisted work of native Africans, but proof that the original inhabitants of the Black Continent were as advanced in their technology as the white race. This viewpoint,

1. *op cit*, p 103.
2. See, for instance, the *Reports* of K. S. R. Robinson and R. Summers for the Rhodesian Commission for the Preservation of Natural and Historical Monuments.

often political in origin, claims that the extant studies of African history are all suspect because they have all been written by colour-prejudiced white men. No doubt disciplined archaeologists like Randall-MacIver and Gertrude Caton-Thompson would dismiss these charges as nonsense as far as their work was concerned. On the other hand, bias is inherent in the argument that since no black South African nation progressed even as far as inventing the arch, none was capable of constructions as architecturally sophisticated as the great Elliptical Enclosure or Temple at Zimbabwe. And if the Enclosure belongs to some period between the sixteenth and nineteenth centuries, then the tribe who built it – undoubtedly with the aid of slaves – could well have employed either Arab, Indian, or Portuguese architects to design and supervise the construction.

And the purpose of these massive structures at Zimbabwe? Again, the experts can give us no positive answers, and how can they when there is nothing in the nature of either a written record or a positive tradition concerning the history of the place? The spokesmen of the various tribes and clans who passed through this region only gave the historians contradictory statements, one man saying, for instance, that a people called the Makaranga paid Arabs to build these places for them to worship their ancestral spirits in; and another asserting that the ruins were built to fight in, but not by Arabs. In general, the local natives have never been able to elucidate the mystery, while the specialists for their part admit they can only guess at the function of the main buildings and the date on which they were built. Here is a table of the datings by the principal experts:

Excavator	*Builders*	*approx. date*
Karl Mauch (1871)	Israelites	950 BC
Theodore Bent ⎱(1890)	Himyarites	2000–1100 BC
Robert Swan ⎰		
Dr Karl Peters (1892)	Egyptians	1450 BC
Dr Heinrich Schlichter (1893)	Babylonians	1100 BC
R. N. Hall (1900)	South Arabians Phoenicians	2000–1100 BC
Dr Randall-MacIver (1905)	Africans	medieval AD 1300–1500
Miss Caton-Thompson (1929)	Africans, but possibly with the help of alien architects	AD 800–1600
K. S. R. Robinson (1958)	Shona-speaking peoples	AD 50–1850

Differences between the earliest and latest estimated date of the foundations of Zimbabwe, nearly 4,000 years. Number of nationalities claimed to have been the builders, six.

After a time, guessing becomes so confusing that it seems pointless to pursue it farther. One may as well stay with the simplest theory: that Zimbabwe was the religious capital of a once wealthy and powerful African tribal group who erected these stone structures probably during the late Middle Ages, possibly with the technical advice of Arab architects. But ask who that nation was, and why its people built these monuments, and how they found enough labour to move and position nearly a million granite blocks, and no definitive answer will be vouchsafed, for the people who built the 'Acropolis' have vanished as though they never existed. Unfortunately there is probably not a single black Rhodesian now living who can enlighten us on these matters; and even if there were, it is highly unlikely that he would confide in a white man. In this respect, the archaeologist Mr K. S. R. Robinson who was working in Rhodesia until quite recently sums up the almost insuperable difficulties of communicating with Africans about their past. He writes:

> I am not a good linguist, nor are my methods of approach such as would commend themselves to some social anthropologists. As a collector of native legends my only recommendations are that I am usually regarded as harmlessly mad by my informants . . . It is probable that the natives who were in the country at the time of occupation viewed with the greatest suspicion any European making inquiries about the habitations of their ancestors. This attitude is less in evidence to-day, but there is often a distinct lowering of the voice and evasiveness of manner betrayed when discussing the old inhabitants of the ruins . . . Zimbabwe was probably the most venerated [of the ancestral places] and therefore not to be spoken about.[1]

In contrast to the African reticence, European travellers and archaeologists have been speaking about this lost city for just over 100 years, often with discordant voices. But everyone who has visited or studied these extraordinary ruins must agree on at least one thing: 'the mystery of Zimbabwe is the mystery which lies in the still pulsating heart of native Africa'.[2]

1. K. S. R. Robinson, *Khami Ruins. Report on Excavations . . . 1947–1955*, Cambridge: University Press, 1959, p 159.
2. Caton-Thompson, *op cit*, p 199.

Part 4
The Americas

Copán
Sites of the principal Maya cities
The Maya civilization flourished from 200 AD to 1550 in southern Mexico and Central America
GULF OF MEXICO
GULF OF CAMPECHE
YUCATAN
Merida
Chichen Itzá
Cobá
Itzá
Campeche
Mani
Carmen
CARIBBEAN SEA
Barrier Reef
Belize City
Palenque
Uaxactún
BELIZE (British Honduras)
Tikal
Holmul
Nakum
GULF OF HONDURAS
Yaxchilan
MEXICO
Naranjo
S. Cristobal de las Casas
S. Pedro Sula
GUATEMALA
HONDURAS
COPAN
Guatemala City
Tegucigalpa
Mazatenango
Sta. Ana
EL SALVADOR
S. Salvador
PACIFIC OCEAN
0 20 100 200 miles
50 100 300 km

Copán

There are certain historical sites – cities like Pompeii, for instance, and even the Roman legion camps adjacent to Hadrian's Wall – which the perceptive traveller can, if only in imagination, people with those who lived and died there. In other words, such places, however remote from our world, still retain a human quality which enables us to peer through the mists of time to an age long since gone by. But Copán, the Maya capital of Honduras, is – on first sight at least – no such place.

For Copán gives the Western-oriented observer a curious sense of strangeness, of other-worldliness, which is summed up by the American explorer John Lloyd Stephens, who first saw it in 1839 after the city had disappeared from the records.

> The city was buried in forest [he writes], and entirely hidden from sight. Little did the citizens imagine that the time would come when their works would perish, their race be extinct, their city a desolation and the abode of reptiles, a ruin for strangers to gaze at and wonder by what manner of men it had once been inhabited.[1]

We can understand Stephens's incredulity as he clambered through the undergrowth and every now and then came face

1. John Lloyd Stephens, *Incidents of Travel in Central America, Chiapas, and Yucatan,* edited by Richard L. Predmore, New Brunswick: Rutgers University Press, 1949, p 81.

to face with the grim-visaged statues of Maya gods who had not been seen or heard of since the conquistadores destroyed them along with their creators. The Spanish soldiers, and particularly their priests, were so incredulous, in fact, that they made no effort to comprehend these Indian civilizations which they actually saw in full operation; and it is no use condemning them for their obtuseness, since their minds were fettered by the religious and social beliefs of their time, just as ours are. After all, these men landed in the Americas, thinking that they were in the Orient, and their imaginations were full of the fantasies and imagery of the East. They were looking for fabulous cities described by Marco Polo and even for fountains of eternal youth; and their ideas of government and society did not range beyond the feudal relationships of sixteenth-century Spain. How could they be expected to explain the political, social, and religious systems of a New World in the terminology suited to the Old? And even for us to-day, after a century and more of the rediscovery and reconstruction of the pre-Columbian Indian cultures, a place like Copán strikes us – one might say almost instinctively – as strangely as it did the conquistadores.

The facts first. Copán and the other Maya – or for that matter Aztec and Inca – cities were not built as urban communities at all, but as centres for religious and civic ceremonies and hence their eeriness; and secondly, the Maya were a people whose beliefs and practices are at once weird and repulsive to a twentieth-century man. Admittedly human sacrifice to which these Indian cultures were committed is common to all primitive religions, including the Judaeo-Christian cults. The potential sacrifice of Isaac by his father on the one hand and the crucifixion of Jesus on the other are indicative of the sanguinary nature of the Semitic gods, all of whom demanded constant appeasement. The Aztecs, Incas, and Mayas had many such monstrous deities whose attributes were as outlandish as their names; and these gods were said to demand human victims to keep them propitious. So much we can dimly comprehend, but where these Indians appal us to-day, as they did the rough and tough Spanish soldiers of the 1500s is in the manner of their sacrifices: namely, the tearing out of the heart of a living man, woman, or child; holding up the bleeding organ for the delectation of the god; and finally devouring the flesh of the corpse. In short, these Indians were anthropophagi, and cannibalism, whether for dietary or religious purposes, is, and always has been, instinctively offensive to civilized people.

It is this aspect of the Maya culture which lingers in the mind as the visitor makes the rounds of the ruins of Copán and is lectured on the subject of the great hieroglyphic staircase and the mathematical and astrological achievements of the Indian tribe who occupied most of Honduras from the third to the eighth century AD. Copán, in fact, was the second largest of the Maya cities, spread out over seventy-five acres, and, as the undoubted capital of the nation, a showplace, then as now, on account of its temples, pyramids, and such-like impressive structures. It is, indeed, the undoubted brilliance of the Maya architecture which has, to some extent, blinded the experts and confused the laymen, so that a great deal of what modern writers have to say (in contrast with those who actually saw the people who built these cities) is often a eulogy rather than a true account, and the reason might be either that these Indian civilizations simply cannot be assessed by our Western-oriented standards; or the current trend to sentimentalize about primitive peoples; or, again, the contemporary tendency to explain the unknown in terms smacking of science-fiction.

One likes, therefore, to go back to where a study of Copán

begins, namely to the discoverer of the city, John Lloyd Stephens, a nineteenth-century American traveller who was certainly not burdened with the academic minutiae of the experts or distracted by the banal observations of official guides.

John Lloyd Stephens was a born 'globe-trotter'. At the age of twenty-nine, he opted out of the law which he was practising in New York and set out for the Mediterranean. His travels in no sense resembled a 'package tour', for Stephens, like all the lone travellers of his time, was prepared to see the world the hard way. Indeed, there was no other way of seeing it. And so, disguised as a Turkish merchant called 'Abdel Hasis', he left Cairo mounted on a camel to cross the Sinai en route to Petra. His guide to the 'rose-red city' was the Bedouin sheikh El Alouin who ended by cheating him of all the cash he possessed. But for Stephens the vexation was worth it. He was at last standing where only travellers like Burckhardt, Leigh, Bankes, Irby, Mangles, the Marquis de La Borde, and Maurice-Adolph Linant had stood (and written their names on the back wall of the Treasury!). He was the first American to reach Petra.

The narrative of his travels in Egypt, Arabia, and the Holy Land, so unassuming and so amusingly written, deservedly became a best-seller, and John Lloyd Stephens, 'the wonderful Arabian traveller', as Herman Melville calls him, became in turn a dedicated explorer. Reviewing the unexplored regions of the world as they appeared to historians and cartographers in the early decades of the last century, the young explorer (he was thirty-three years old) now chose as his particular domain the almost unknown and unmapped countries of Central America; and he did so after consultations with the historian Francis L. Hawks who drew his attention to reports by European travellers of lost cities in Mexico and Yucatan. Stephens was already something of a celebrity following the publication of his first book, *Incidents of Travel in Egypt, Arabia Petraea, and the Holy Land* (1837) and its successor, *Incidents of Travel in Greece, Turkey, Russia, and Poland* (1838), and he evidently had little difficulty in getting his new project sponsored by his publishers, Harper & Brothers, as well as by collectors ready to buy any artefacts he could bring back from the jungle. In addition, he was fortunate to live in an age when governments encouraged scholarship through the medium of diplomacy, as a glance at the extra-official activities of so many British, French, German, and American consuls abroad will show. Thus Stephens, though without any diplomatic experience, seemed to have had no difficulty in persuading President Van Buren to send him on an official mission as the United States Minister to Central America. The only reservation of the State Department, in fact, was that no one in Washington really knew whether a Central American government actually existed; and if so, where it was located, what was its capital, and who its president. But Stephens had taken on the assignment on the assumption that an ambassador's person was sacrosanct and his prestige such that he could travel anywhere he wanted without let or hindrance, even in the uncharted territories of Guatemala and Honduras. He was, as we shall see, very mistaken.

Even when flying high above the great mountains and dense forests of Yucatan, one can visualize Stephens slogging his way overland with his companion and colleague, the English architect-archaeologist, Frederick Catherwood, and his guide, the mulatto Augustin. The three men with their baggage-mules stopped at the villages and old Spanish-American towns along the tracks they followed *en route* to Copán, and nothing that Stephens saw or experienced was wasted. It is, indeed, his description of everyday events which makes his book so readable even to-day, for he is never pompous, never indulges in long purple passages as so many Victorian travel writers were inclined to do. His *Incidents*, in short, is a very personal narrative, so that one is almost present at the alarming yet hilarious incident of his arrest by the soldiers of General Cascara, one of three contenders for the presidency of the self-styled 'Central American Republic'.

> The band of cowardly ruffians stood with their hands on their swords and machetes, and two assassin-looking scoundrels sat on a bench with muskets on their shoulders, the muzzles pointing within three feet of my breast . . . I demanded that we be set at liberty immediately and allowed to proceed on our journey without further molestation, adding that we should, of course, report to my own government and that at Guatemala City the manner in which we had been treated. Not to mince matters, Mr. Catherwood signed the note as Secretary and, having no official seal with me, we sealed it unobserved by anybody with a new American half dollar . . .[1]

Stephens at last reached the ruins he had travelled 1,500 miles to see, only to discover that he was apparently to be denied even a walk through the Maya city by the owner of the land on which it was built, one Don José Maria, described as 'tall and well dressed – that is to say, his cotton shirt and pantaloons were clean'. After protracted negotiations, the explorer, in fact, had to purchase the ruins, lock, stock, and barrel, before he and his colleague could begin their work of surveying the site. With his usual humour and eye for detail, Stephens describes how, clad in his full diplomatic regalia of a Panama hat soaked with rain and spotted with mud, and wearing his 'diplomatic' coat with its profusion of brass buttons, he purchased the Maya city of Copán, with everything it con-

1. *op cit*, pp 62, 63.

tained, for fifty dollars. 'There was never any difficulty about the price,' he writes. 'I offered the sum for which Don José Maria thought me only a fool.'[1]

It was a droll transaction and perhaps one of the strangest ever made, because shortly afterwards the Maya artefacts – particularly hieroglyphic tablets, stelae, and the sculptures – were to be bought by Western museums for astronomical sums, until they became to all intents and purposes priceless: in other words, Stephens had bought a veritable gold-mine for fifty dollars. He was not unmindful of his *coup*, for he writes that, as he wandered excitedly over his newly acquired real estate, discovering new treasures every few yards, he felt 'a pang of regret that we must abandon the idea of carrying away any materials for antiquarian speculation'. By 'antiquarian speculation', he meant that he had various business transactions in mind and the 'pang of regret' refers to the difficulties he foresaw in transporting large monuments through the jungle back to the United States.

We see Stephens here in the character of a Yankee businessman, for in addition to his career as traveller and writer, he was to become a very energetic president of the Panama Railroad Company among other things. His colleague Frederick Catherwood, on the other hand, was far more interested in the exceedingly complex problem of drawing the stelae, or 'idols' as they were called, than of sizing up their market value. Catherwood was a true artist as well as a very competent archaeologist, and it was really he who gave Copán to the world in the shape of his beautiful plans and drawings which have never been surpassed. And under what conditions this romantic Englishman who was to drown at sea while crossing the Atlantic in 1854 worked! Shivering with 'the fever', almost knee-deep in mud, obliged to wear gloves

1. *ibid*, p 112.

because of the continuous attack of the mosquitoes, he drew exquisitely accurate pictures of the monuments of Copán, and nobody since has ever captured the wonder of the lost city with such sensitivity as well as realism as this fever-stricken artist.

One could hardly expect Stephens's straightforward prose to rival Catherwood's drawings, but the two men between them could be said to have given Copán to the world as Burckhardt gave us Petra: that is, the picture of a lost city before its mystery was made prosaic by tourism. Of course, the place they saw and the conditions under which they saw it no longer exist, and the visitor to-day must not expect to see the procession of monkeys through the tree-tops or hear the chattering of parrots that the two explorers saw and heard. What we see to-day is a Mayan urban site painstakingly restored by a hundred years of dedicated archaeology and not the lost city seen by the Spanish Justice of the Royal Audience of Guatemala, for instance, who came across it in 1576 and described 'the superb edifices which could never have been built by the natives'.

The Justice means, of course, that the contemporary Indians of the province could not have erected such splendid monuments, and he was mystified as to who had built them. The mystery remains. How did the Maya learn to design and build great structures in dressed stone when their descendants could build nothing more substantial than a wattle hut? How could they invent a calendrical system so precise as to enable them to predict eclipses of the sun? How could they invent a system of writing when the North American Indians had not even reached the stage of pictograms? Where did they acquire the engineering skills to build great roads which criss-crossed the country? And so forth . . .

The answer to nearly all these and other related questions has been partially found by intensive research, and in some respects the Maya are no more and no less mysterious than, say, the Etruscans. There is certainly an enormous literature on the subject, both scholarly and popular, and no aspect of their lives and achievements has been left unstudied. There remain 'puzzles', however. Why did the Maya, who seem to have been so brilliant in mathematics and astronomy, never invent, or certainly never put into use, the wheel employed throughout millennia of Western civilization? And why did they build roads running in a straight line between towns even to the extent of avoiding detours around swamps and lakes? These roads, moreover, were built with quite advanced engineering skills, being thirty feet wide, set on strong foundations, and walled on each side with roughly dressed stones. They seem unnecessarily elaborate constructions just to cater for porters and pedestrians in a country where horses, carts, and beasts of burden were unknown. And why, again, in view of their advanced social organization did they not evolve from a hierarchical society into something resembling a democracy?

In trying to answer such questions – which are actually common to a great many defunct civilizations – we would be wise to avoid the mistake made by the old Spanish priests on the one hand and the modern experts on the other: that is, of attempting to interpret the Maya culture by contemporary standards. For the fact is that we really cannot enter into the minds of any truly theocentric people, since religion, in the context of a constant awareness of a god, or gods, plays no significant role in our daily lives. Our God is faceless and incorporeal. The Maya had dozens of gods, all with faces and forms and all as real as our temporal rulers. On the whole, one could say that these divinities were as unlovable as their names were unpronounceable, and why even a theocentric people should abase themselves to such monsters is as incomprehensible to us as their belief that the world rested on the back of a crocodile floating in a vast pond. One would have thought that somebody would have asked why the crocodile put up with this burden. But the Maya never questioned either their cosmologists or their theologians, so we cannot expect to understand what all their mummery was about, except that it sustained and perpetuated a system based on the divine right of the priesthood. Many gods, moreover, required many priests to serve them, and the priests in their turn required many novitiates to share their responsibilities.

The Indian gods, we know, demanded continual sacrifices, particularly of humans whose blood was thought to give them the strength required to perform their duties. The Maya, and more particularly the Aztec, methods of providing blood to nourish the god were especially revolting. For instance, whereas we might accept the argument that a sacrificial victim died for the communal good, it is hard to see why he, or she, should have to be hurled down the steps of the pyramid from top to bottom, then have the heart torn out, the body flayed, and the choicest limbs devoured by the top officials. This seems to be overdoing one's respect for the Almighty and explains why the old Greeks very early in their history refused to be tyrannized by gods like Apollo the Destroyer and turned him into Apollo the Healer.

Something of this bewilderment as to what these people really believed is bound to be experienced by the thoughtful visitor to Copán as he stands in the Eastern Court, considered the most sacred part of the acropolis. Here he is in the presence of still another mystery, the celebrated Hieroglyphic Stairway rising to almost 100 feet and displaying on its steps some of the strangest communications left us by the inhabitants of a vanished world – 2,500 engraved messages which at first suggest that the Maya, like the ancient Egyptians, had recorded their history in symbols carved into the walls of their monuments.

But as one would expect with these Indians, an answer to a question is never simple and direct. Did the Maya invent a written language? Yes and no. Yes in the sense that they could transmit simple messages by means of symbols; no in the sense that they had neither an alphabet nor a syllabic system of writing. They used glyphs to communicate such facts as they considered worth recording, a development, it is true, upon the most primitive form of written communication, like that found, for instance, on the walls of European caves or the *abris* of African cliff-settlements where some fact or event is presented in picture form. But the Maya glyphs are still pictures – usually of their gods and animals – strung together to produce a simple statement provided the reader knows the code. To some extent, we use glyphs ourselves: in other words, conventionalized signs strung out along our roads, a child bouncing a ball for *School*, a leaping stag for *Deer liable to cross the road*, a diagonal band through a bicycle for *Cyclists not allowed*, and so forth. Such picture graphs are wholly adequate to express simple statements of fact, but quite inappropriate for rendering abstract ideas. How can one draw a picture to express the abstraction 'to know', for instance?

Certain people did discover how to convey ideas by means of signs even before the invention of the alphabet, the Sumerians, Egyptians, Babylonians, and Hittites among them. In other words, these people had a written language in which they could describe all aspects of their culture, intangible as well as material phenomena. The Maya had no such script and were limited to what is in point of fact an endless series of dates for the commencement and completion of their buildings. These dates are written in glyphs or signs for each of the days, months, and years of the Maya calendar; and we know the precise meaning of each glyph thanks to a history of Yucatan written about 1560, quite soon after the conquest, by Diego de Landa, the second Bishop of Yucatan. The bishop gives a detailed account of the calendar and illustrates his remarks with drawings of the signs for the days, months, and years.

Maya writing, in brief, tells us next to nothing of the political or social history of the people. Even so, we can almost go so far as to say that we practically know all there is to know about the actual lives of the Maya, their appearance, beliefs, customs, and the most important events in their history. A visit to Copán explains why. All around are the sculptures, carvings, temples, and civic buildings which tell much of the story. One can certainly see by looking around at the sculptured stones, notably the famous stelae which Frederick Catherwood drew so beautifully, what the Mayan looked like: sloping forehead, almond-shaped eyes, large nose, drooping lower lip, receding chin; elaborate headdress, short tunic; and many ornaments covering his back and chest. One can see how he travelled in a hammock-like litter carried by two porters and accompanied by his favourite dog. One can see him in battle, in the temple, and in his palace. And most important, what was not depicted in stone was enshrined in tradition which the priests who accompanied the conquistadores managed to record despite their abhorrence of a culture which sanctified cannibalism.

In fact, there is so much information of one sort and another, that the writing of histories of the Maya never stops, and each year new facts and new interpretations add to the document-ation. For in addition to the scholars who assiduously dig away on the still-unexcavated sites which dot the Yucatan and Honduras landscape, the amateurs continue to follow in the footsteps of their once-celebrated predecessor, Augustus Le Plongeon who appeared upon the scene in the very early days of exploration.[1] Dr Le Plongeon, a splendidly-bearded

1. See James Wellard, *The Search for Lost Worlds*, London & Sydney: Pan Books, 1975.

Franco-American physician, not only dedicated himself (and Mrs Le Plongeon) to the cause of the Maya but to demonstrating that these people were descendants of the Atlanteans whose strange story is told by Plato in the two dialogues, *Timaeus* and *Critias*. Le Plongeon had no difficulty in proving his theory, since he claimed to be able to read the Maya texts 'by means of the ancient hieratic Maya alphabet discovered by me'.[1] This alphabet, he states, was essentially the same as 'the Egyptian Hieratic alphabet according to Messrs Champollion le Jeune and Bunsen'. But assuming some philologists were prepared at least to consider this possibility, even Dr Le Plongeon's most fervent admirers had difficulty in swallowing his assertion that the Maya were using a telegraphic system complete with telegraph wires, some 10,000 years ago. In short, the Indians had invented wireless telegraphy during the reign of the beautiful Queen Moo, daughter of King Can and elder sister and wife of King Coh. The doctor said that he had found the wires projecting from a lintel over a door at Chichen Itza where, aided by Mrs Le Plongeon, he dug around and made moulds of sculptures which he presented to the Metropolitan Museum of Art. The Museum greatly offended him by depositing the casts in the cellar on the grounds that 'the public were not interested in such things'.

But Dr Le Plongeon pressed on with his Atlantean theory of the origin of the Maya and finally found a certain fame and an international following. He passes on the torch with these words:

> After twelve years of incessant labors and great hardships, unaided by any government or scientific society, having to encounter opposition and surmount countless difficulties

1. Augustus Le Plongeon, *Sacred Mysteries among the Maya and the Quiches 11,500 years ago*, New York: Robert Macoy, 1896, p xi.

placed maliciously in our way by those whose duty it should have been to afford us all protection, robbed of our finds by the Mexican Government, Mrs. Le Plongeon and myself, after saving from destruction many important documents and relics, have at last found a key that will unlock the door of that chamber of mysteries. Shall it be allowed to remain closed much longer? We have lifted in part at least, the veil that has hung so long over the history of mankind in America in remote ages. Shall it be allowed to fall again? Will no efforts be made by American students, by men of wealth and leisure in the United States to remove it altogether?[1]

So, part of the fascination as well as the mystery of Copán is the effect it has had on its visitors, on the experts as on the amateurs; for the place and the civilization it personified have become the semi-private preserve of pedants on the one hand and the playground of cranks on the other. A great deal of heat if not of light has been generated by both parties during the 150 years or so since the first American to see the ruins came out of the forests of Honduras. Arguments as to whether the ancient Maya were Mongols, Chinese, Polynesians, Atlanteans, Egyptians, and so forth still rumble around the academies. Denials that they knew the wheel continue to enrage their admirers. Claims that their script was Sumerian, Egyptian, and even Greek are the basis of many a translation of the three books which survived the Spanish holocaust. Hence there is plenty of material for the tourist to ponder upon as he climbs about the ruins of Copán; but when at last he comes to leave to take the car or bus back to his rest-house, he will certainly still be asking the question that no one, neither expert nor amateur, has been able to answer: why was

1. *op cit*, pp 152–3.

a city of the size and splendour of Copán suddenly abandoned? Excess population and shortage of food, say some experts. Failure of the agricultural system, say others. Others again suggest epidemics of diseases like yellow fever or malaria. And there is one school of thought which proposes that the peasants and serfs grew rebellious because of the exactions and injustices placed upon them in the name of religion and finally revolted and overthrew the hierarchy.

The question has been asked over and over again wherever we find a great abandoned city, once the capital of an empire. It was, indeed, the same question that John Lloyd Stephens asked as he rode away on that late spring day in 1840. And he answers:

> Nor shall I offer any conjecture in regard to the people who built it; or to the time when, or the means by which it was depopulated to become a desolation and ruin; or as to whether it fell by the sword, or famine, or pestilence. The trees that shroud it may have sprung from the blood of its slaughtered inhabitants; they may have perished howling with hunger; or pestilence, like the cholera, may have piled its streets with the dead and driven for ever the feeble remnants from their homes . . .[1]

Stephens did not, in fact, hang around Copán waiting for the answers to these questions to come to him from the stones. Leaving Mr Catherwood to carry on with his drawings (and nearly to die of 'the fever'), the young American set forth again on his journey, and the next we hear of him is his meeting with the fair-haired sister of Don Clementino, the owner of a large *hacienda* across the Guatemalan border from Honduras and Copán. She was about sixteen, and when she leaves in her party

1. *op cit*, p 124.

dress to go to a wedding, sitting side-saddle on a mule which also carried 'the happy young gallant' who escorted her and turned her face so that her lips almost touched her companion's, Stephens, the discoverer of Copán, remarks: 'I would have given all the honors of diplomacy for his place.'

This, then, is where we leave John Lloyd Stephens and his Copán, noting that an explorer able to write like that – with so much sense of fun and *joie de vivre* – deserved to sell his *Incidents of Travel* by the tens of thousands between 1841 and 1871, when the twelfth and last edition was printed. Indeed, it is sad that such a splendid book, being out of print and available now only in the national libraries, is no longer read; but this, of course, is the fate of almost all the Victorian travellers' tales. Yet even among a company as distinguished as Burckhardt, Barth, Livingstone, Burton, and Stanley, the American still stands out not only for his courage, which was admittedly common to them all, but for his special brand of charm and humour. From the more serious viewpoint of scholarship, on the other hand, his contribution to Mayan studies is incalculable, and not without reason has he been called the Father of Mayan archaeology. His accounts of Copán and other lost cities of Central America were the first of their kind and remained together with Catherwood's drawings the only record we have of many monuments now lost or destroyed.

In a more general way, John Lloyd Stephens's narratives illuminated what could very easily have become just another humdrum reportage of ruins, and ruins a-plenty were being discovered all the time all over the world. Copán was different. It was very special, since very little of archaeological or, for that matter, historical interest had been discovered in the Americas up to his day – certainly nothing to compare with the wonders of cities like Petra. With the publication of *Incidents of Travel in South America*, the Americans felt that they at last had their own Petra, with their own ancient history,

The Elizabethan settlers on Roanoke Island were probably massacred by the local Indians. John White, Governor of the settlement, made this watercolour drawing of an Indian soothsayer

The mysterious Dare Stone – real or fake? The inscription shown reads: 'Ananias Dare & Virginia went hence Unto Heaven 1591. Anye English- man shew John White Govr Via'

The mysterious prehistoric (Late Neolithic) temples on the island of
Malta, at Hagar Qim: nothing yet known explains what gods were
worshipped, who built the temples, or why they vanished utterly

all awaiting exploration and study by their own scholars. The result was a surge of interest in archaeology and history which has continued to flow through many channels of the intellectual life of America ever since.

This, then, was John Lloyd Stephens's main achievement: he not only discovered Copán, but gave it back to the world in such a way that those who have no hope of ever setting foot there can still enjoy it from the comfort of their armchair. And the Copán they will visit is magical.

> The only sound that disturbed the quiet of this buried city was the noise of the monkeys moving among the tops of the trees and the cracking of dry branches broken by their weight. They moved over our head in long and swift processions, forty or fifty at a time. Some with little ones wrapped in their long arms walked out to the end of a bough and, holding on with their hind feet or a curl of the tail, sprang to the branch of the next tree; with a noise like a current of wind, they passed on into the depths of the forest . . . They seemed like the wandering spirits of the departed race guarding the ruins of their former habitations. For the city was desolate. It lay before us like a shattered bark in the midst of the ocean, her masts gone, her name effaced, her crew perished, and none to tell whence she came, to whom she belonged, or what caused her destruction.[1]

1. *op cit*, pp 79, 124.

The City of Raleigh

The English Colonies in North America from the founding of the city of Raleigh, 1587 to the founding of Philadelphia, 1681

The City of Raleigh

What, we may ask, induced those 117 people to leave their quiet English homes one morning in the summer of 1587 and to set out in three small ships for a world as alien to them as the moon is to us?

Well, perhaps the Reverend Daniel Price preaching from St Paul's Cross in 1607 gives us the answer. The New World to which these immigrants were going

> equalizes Tyrus for colours, Basan for woods, Persia for oils, Arabia for spices, Spain for silks, Narcis for shipping, Netherlands for fish, Pomona for fruit, Babylon for corn, besides the abundance of mulberries, minerals, rubies, pearls, gems, grapes, deer, fowls, drugs for physic, herbs for food, roots for colours, ashes for soap, timber for building, pastures for feeding, rivers for fishing . . .[1]

Such was the concept of Virginia held by those who had never been out of England, and it is self-evident that people who would believe that sort of twaddle would gladly gamble their lives on the venture sponsored by Sir Walter Raleigh and his Virginia Company. But it was not deliberate deception on the part of the Rev. Price, but rather *naïveté* which led him to hold forth like a salesman for a quack medicine. In fact, the first colonists to return from the New World, the French Huguenots

1. Daniel Price, *The Marchant*: A Sermon Preached at Paules Cross on Sunday the 24 of August, 1607, J. Barnes, Oxford, 1608, p 17.

who had settled in Florida in 1562, were already spinning tales of jewel-mines which could be approached only by night on account of the brilliance of the precious stones.

Thus in 1587 Raleigh and his co-directors of the Virginia Company had no difficulty in recruiting a group of farmers and craftsmen, with the wives and children of several of them, to be transported across the Atlantic to an island off the coast of North America which early explorers called Wingandacoa[1] and afterwards Virginia in honour of the English Queen. The colonists were offered 200 acres of rich land for only twelve pounds and ten shillings, a most tempting offer to an English tenant farmer; and spurred on by promises of an easy life and a quick fortune, the emigrants were prepared to face the un-known – even the weird monsters and terrifying natural phenomena which the explorers of the New World described along with tales of rubies and diamonds scattered about on the seashore. The promoters, then, found no dearth of willing and able volunteers: the company that set out in 1587 to establish the City of Raleigh on Roanoke Island, Virginia, consisted of the best type of English rustics – sober, hard-working country folk whose very names evoke memories of busy county towns and quiet villages – John Sampson, Humphrey Newton, Emma Merrimoth, Jane Mannering.

The leader of the expedition was John White of London, gentleman, who was appointed 'Governor of the City of Raleigh in Virginia'. Very little is known about John White except what he tells us himself in his *Journal* of his voyage to Virginia in 1587 and the *Report* of his last voyage in 1590. We can see that he was a typical Elizabethan – adventurous, some-thing of an opportunist, and above all, versatile – a minor example in his way of the new Renaissance Man. His profession,

---

1. Actually a Cherokee word meaning 'You wear fine clothes' – a linguistic misunderstanding caused by the Indian's ignorance of English, and vice versa.

in so far as he had one, was surveying. But his principal talent was for painting, and it is to John White that we owe the first drawings of American Indians and of the flora and fauna of the New World – a collection of seventy-five exquisitely painted water colours now in the British Museum. He also drew the 'carte of all the coast of Virginia' which formed the basis of the subsequent 'Map of Virginia' (1612) of Captain John Smith.

It is also Governor White who gives us an eye-witness account of the disastrous attempt to build a city and found a colony in the New World, only ninety-three years after Columbus had discovered land and thirty-five years before the Pilgrim Fathers reached Massachusetts. It is not difficult to see why this attempt, one of the most interesting and curious events in British colonial history, was doomed to fail. Indeed, failure was inherent in both the methods and the conduct of the organizers themselves, men whose names are now revered as national heroes and whose exploits are the very stuff of British naval history – Hawkins, Grenville, Gilbert, Drake, Raleigh. Yet all these great men were not so much explorers as buccaneers, and it was greed for Spanish gold that motivated their great voyages far more than the desire to plant British colonies in the New World. In fact, Roanoke Island was initially chosen as a useful base from which the British privateers could operate against the Spanish galleons, though it is true that by 1587, Raleigh with only three years left of his grant 'to discover, search, find, and view such heathen and barbarous lands not actually possessed of any Christian Prince, nor inhabited by Christian people' decided that he had better plant a civilian colony on the island in order to protect his monopoly.

But, as we shall see, he had left it too late. The obsession with privateering and the hope of quick profits to be gained by preying upon the Spanish galleons returning from South

America laden with treasure conflicted with the more prosaic and less remunerative task of revictualling the overseas settlements; and in 1587 the threat of the Armada was to lead Raleigh and his fellow-directors practically to abandon the little company of colonists clinging to a fragment of land 3,000 miles from home. For three years from 1587 to 1590 there was no contact with Roanoke Island – no contact, no message, and, when the relief party finally did reach the Island, no sign at all of those 117 Englishmen and women who had built the City of Raleigh – except, of course, for that one mysterious word they had carved on a tree: CROATOAN. The mystery of the Lost Colony was born. It has never been solved.

The story begins with the assembling at Portsmouth in early April, 1587 of three expeditionary ships, the largest of which was a galleon called *Lion*, of 120 tons. The small Elizabethan galleon was a square-rigged, three-masted ship with a high square turret in the bows (hence the nautical term fore*castle*), a low waist amidships, and a high poop in the stern. Such warships carried an assortment of guns, including cannon, culverins, basilisks, sakers, minions, falconets, serpentines, and robinets. These crude weapons fired iron shot and shrapnel when the gunners could get them to work, but generally speaking naval battles were close encounters in which the crews fired hand-guns of one sort or another or relied on bows and arrows, morris pikes, bills, darts, and lime pots.

The *Lion*, then, was the flagship of the Virginia colonists' fleet and carried the majority of the passengers under the usual cramped and comfortless conditions of sailing ships from time immemorial. The second vessel, name unrecorded, was a small craft of only fifty tons known as a flyboat, a term for a fast shallow-draft boat used for the rapid transport of goods in the sixteenth and seventeenth centuries. The third boat was a pinnace, a light boat only thirty feet in length and dependent upon sails and oars. This little fleet set sail from Portsmouth on 26 April 1587, and to the passengers it must have been the most dramatic moment of their lives as anchors were weighed and the crews of the boats began their weird chanting.

> Then the mariners began to hoist up the sail, crying 'Heisan! Heisan! Vorsa! Vorsa! Vou! Vou! One long pull! One long pull! More power! More power! Young blood! Young blood! More mud! More mud! False flesh! False flesh! That! That! That! That! There! There! There! There! Yellow hair! Yellow hair! Hips bare! Hips bare! To him all! To him all! Viddefullis all! Viddefullis all! Great and small! Great and small! One and all! One and all! Heisan! Heisan! Now each make fast theirs.'[1]

From Portsmouth the fleet sailed to Plymouth, and on 8 May set course for Virginia via the West Indies, the customary route to the Americas throughout the sixteenth century in order to pick up the north-east trade winds and the north-flowing Gulf Stream. From Puerto Rico they sailed up the coast of Florida, the Carolinas, and so to the chain of islands off the coast of what was then 'Virginia' and is now North Carolina. One of these islands was called Roanoke, and it is difficult to think of a more dangerous landfall even for modern ships furnished with the most sophisticated navigational aids. For Roanoke is one of a chain of low-lying islands forming the Outer Banks of North Carolina. These islands consist of long ramparts of sand bars which change annually under the battering of winds and tides, so much so that buoying the area needs constant attention and navigating through it for

1. *The Complaynt of Scotland*, 1548 . . . with a preliminary dissertation by John Leyden, Edinburgh: Constable, 1801, p 30.

sailing vessels is always hazardous. Inlets and passages between
the islands open and close so that it is now fruitless to try and
determine by which inlet Raleigh's ships entered. For when
we remember that the Elizabethan galleon was square-rigged
and hence unable either to sail close to the wind or manoeuvre
smartly, we wonder how such ships survived the dangers of
uncharted rocks, shoals, sandbanks, and lee-shores, let alone
how they found the channel to Roanoke Island and which
channel they chose. In fact, it was the unsuitability of Roanoke
as an anchorage which was to prove in part the reason for the
failure of the colony to thrive. In short, the anchorage was
difficult to locate and dangerous to remain in.

Governor White and the colonists did, however, eventually
arrive at the designated spot where the City of Raleigh was to
be built as the American capital of the incipient British empire.
The landfall was made not without the usual trials and tribulations, including near-shipwreck off the significantly named
Cape Fear. Governor White puts this down to the incompetence
of the Portuguese pilot, Simon Ferdinando. The voyagers went
ashore on the island at sunset, expecting to find fifteen Englishmen who had been left there a year before as an advance party.
There was no sign of life. On the contrary, the bones of one of
the settlers proved that the fifteen had been slain 'by the
savages'. Also, the fort that had been built at the north end of
the island had been destroyed, though the houses clustered
round it remained standing. Governor White's report gives
a strangely moving picture of the desolation in a few words:

> The fort was overgrown with melons [he writes], and
> inside deer were feeding upon them. There was nothing to
> do but to return and give up hope of ever seeing the fifteen
> men alive again.

1. Theodore de Bry, *The New World*, Duell, Sloan & Pearce: New York,
1946, p 158.

The work of building the new town, to be called in honour of Sir Walter the City of Raleigh, now began. The colonists already had several houses ready for occupation – namely, those built by the previous expeditionary force led by Sir Richard Grenville, Raleigh's cousin. In addition to these, they erected further buildings sufficient to accommodate all the settlers and to provide some comforts for the seventeen women and nine children. One of the women, Elinor Dare, daughter of Governor White, was far advanced in her pregnancy and, indeed, was to give birth to a girl a few weeks after landing. The baby, the first white child to be born in North America, was named Virginia, the Virginia Dare who reappears later in this story in strange circumstances.

It would have seemed that having successfully crossed the ocean and having landed at the place they were seeking despite the difficulties, the pioneers would now settle down in comparative peace and safety to establish their colony and gradually to extend its frontiers. But the Elizabethans seldom enjoyed peace and security for long, whether at home, on the high seas, or in their new colonies. Here their violent life-style was bound to lead to confrontation with the aborigines following the inevitable killings of one or several white men. Thus, soon after Governor White's arrival, one of his staff, a man called George Howe, was slain on the seashore by Indians.

> The savages, hidden in the high reeds where they often find the wild deer sleeping, espied Howe wading in the water. He was alone, almost naked, and without any arms save a small forked stick with which he was endeavouring to catch crabs. They [the Indians] wounded him with sixteen arrow-shots. Then they killed him with their wooden swords, beat his head to pieces, and escaped over the water to the mainland.[1]

1. *op cit*, p 159.

From now onwards, the instinct of colonists and natives alike was kill or be killed, and it is futile four centuries later to blame either side – the Indians for defending their homeland or the immigrants for trying to establish theirs.

One can imagine the problems these 117 men, women, and children had to face on Roanoke Island in 1587, and the murder of George Howe on the seashore epitomizes the nature of their difficulties. In short, they were not at all secure and considered themselves with good reason to be continuously threatened by hostile forces – the Indians, the unexplored continent at their backs, and the dangerous coast on which they were semi-stranded. There must also have been severe internal strains which are only hinted at in Governor White's report, though to some extent they are revealed in the curious business of choosing an agent from among their numbers to return to England as their representative. One says curious, first, because it is surprising that so soon after landing they found it necessary to send someone all the way back to England merely to ensure the speedy dispatch of supplies, which one would have thought must surely have been anticipated long before they set sail; and secondly, because nobody was prepared to undertake this assignment. However, we can guess at the reasons from the evidence Governor White provides in his account of the voyage across: the trip was undoubtedly beset by disagreements amounting to outright conspiracy on the part of the master and crew of the flagship *Lion*. White distrusted and, indeed, detested Simon Ferdinando the captain of the *Lion* and pilot for the little fleet. Ferdinando, or Fernandez as he would be called to-day, was a Portuguese master mariner who had emigrated, or deserted, to England. As the Portuguese were the most skilled of European seamen, he was quickly taken up by Sir Francis Walsingham and Sir Humphrey Gilbert as their chief pilot in American waters where piracy was a highly profitable and, indeed, legalized business.

Ferdinando had made several crossings of the Atlantic and, more important, a reconnaissance voyage along the North American coast. His whole attitude to seafaring was that of his age and his employers, so that he must have been disgruntled at having to take on a peaceful assignment like the founding of a colony, and his behaviour on the voyage certainly points to that conclusion. He delayed progress wherever he could, for he was continually on the look-out for easy prizes in the waters of the Indies, whereas he knew that none was to be found off the coast of Virginia. And once he had reached Roanoke Island and had off-loaded the settlers and their now much reduced supplies (reduced because of delays *en route*), he was impatient to get back to England and the serious business of piracy.

And so we sense that there was something of a crisis within a few days of the arrival of the colonists, which quickly came to a head in the controversy over who was to return to England to organize the vital shipments of supplies. As Governor White reports it, his assistants could not, or would not, agree to nominate two of their number for this purpose. They all refused 'save only one which all the other thought not suffici-ent', a reference, no doubt, to the pilot Ferdinando. The argu-ments continued for several weeks, and while it is obvious that everybody was averse to taking the assignment, it is not so obvious why. One can only guess at some of the possible reasons: fear of the trans-Atlantic crossing; fear of not being able to get back again and so losing rights and privileges; and distrust of fellow-adventurers. The reality of the last of these three fears is proven by Governor White's insistence, when he was finally obliged to return himself, that every one of the colonists should sign a bond the text of which he is careful to include in his report:

We, the planters in Virginia, have most earnestly entreated

John White, Governor, to pass into England, though much against his will, promising the safe preserving of all his goods for him at his return to Virginia, so that if any part thereof were spoiled, or lost, they would see it restored to him, or his assigns, whensoever the same should be missed and demanded: which bond, with a testimony under their hands and seals, they forthwith made . . . The copy of this testimony I thought good to set down.[1]

While the colonists were evidently so short of certain supplies that they insisted on Governor White hastening back to England to ensure replenishment of their stocks, it seems probable that the items needed would have been in the nature of weapons and tools, together, of course, with a few comforts like books, clothes, musical instruments, and the beer which was the staple Elizabethan beverage. But the whole business of White's precipitous departure is a puzzle, since we next learn that the Company already had three assistants or factors purposely left behind in England to attend to the needs of the colony; and the possibility arises that the settlers who had 'come to the Governor and with one voice requested him to return himself into England' were dissatisfied with his leadership and intended to elect one of their number to replace him. Their dissatisfaction may have stemmed from the manner in which he allowed the pilot Ferdinando to dally around the West Indies in the hope of capturing a prize; or from some negligence in the quantity and quality of the supplies themselves.

Shortly after Governor White had agreed to return to England, severe gales along the Virginia coast placed the colonists' ships at risk, for they had been anchored on the lee shore of the islands and were in danger of being wrecked. In such conditions ships must put out to sea as soon as they can,

1. *The Roanoke Voyages, 1587–1590*, edited by David Beers Quinn, London: For the Hakluyt Society, 1955, p 534.

and so it was that the *Lion* cut her cables and stood out to the open sea, there to ride out the storm. She was gone, in fact, for seven days. Then, when the wind and sea subsided, she sailed back to the island to pick up Governor White and several members of the crew who had been ashore when she had made her dash for safety. For some reason not explained, the Governor decided to make the homeward passage aboard the little flyboat, which had had half her crew badly incapacitated by an accident while weighing anchor. A spoke of the capstan had suddenly flown off, throwing twelve men on to the deck, and when they tried to control the capstan, two more spokes snapped off, so injuring the sailors that they were unable to raise the anchor and had to cut it loose. These twelve men had been so badly hurt, in fact, that they scarcely had strength to work the ship on the passage. Governor White was lucky to reach the west coast of Ireland after fifty days at sea in view of these conditions which he describes with his usual reticence:

> There arose a storm at Northeast, which for six days ceased not to blow so exceeding that we were driven further in those six than we could recover in thirteen days: in which time other of our sailors began to fall very sick, and two of them died . . . Now we expected nothing but by famine to perish at sea.[1]

But Governor White at last arrived safely home, to make his report to Raleigh and, above all, to arrange for the dispatch of much-needed supplies to the colonists on Roanoke.

In the meantime, how was this little band of 'planters', as they called themselves, faring?

Unfortunately they left no written record of themselves – or, if they did, their manuscripts have not survived. We are forced, therefore, to reconstruct the City of Raleigh and the

1. *op cit*, pp 536–7.

life lived there from various scraps of evidence which contemporary records and recent archaeological excavations provide.

We know that probably 114 people remained on Roanoke after Governor White's departure, and we know their names and a little something about several of them. We know, for instance, that a boy and a girl had already been born, the former's name not recorded, the latter the famous Virginia Dare, daughter of Ananias and Elinor Dare and granddaughter of John White. We know, too, that there were only fourteen families comprising some thirty-six people as against seventy-four bachelors and probably four spinsters. Again, two of the group, listed as 'savages', were Indians who, brought to England in the course of Raleigh's 1584 and 1586 expeditions to Virginia, had been sent back with the new colonists. These two Indians, Manteo and Towaye, and particularly the former, played an important role in the drama of the City of Raleigh, for one of the first enactments of the colonists on settling down was, 'by the commandment of Sir Walter Raleigh', to nominate Manteo Lord of Roanoke and Dosemunkepeue.

The Lord of Roanoke belonged to the Carolina Algonkian tribe; his hunting-grounds were the island of Croatoan in what is to-day the Carolina Outer Banks. He had been carried off as a hostage in 1584 and had spent three years in England in the household of Sir Walter learning English and being exhibited as a propagandist for colonization. His fellow-Indian, Towaye, had probably been captured by Sir Richard Grenville in the 1586 expedition to Virginia, and he, too, was used as an interpreter. But while Manteo became very much involved in the affairs of the colony and, indeed, was described by Governor White as one who 'behaved himself towards us as a most faithful Englishman', Towaye seems to have played no part in the venture. He may even have returned to England with the Governor, for there is some evidence that the 'Indian' entered in the Parish Register of Bideford in North Devon as having been buried in the Parish churchyard on 7 April 1589 was none other than Towaye.

It is not difficult to imagine what the settlers' lives were like after the fleet that had brought them to Roanoke had sailed away on the morning of 27 August 1587. Thanks to the good offices of Manteo, Lord of Roanoke, they were temporarily at peace with the neighbouring Indians and so were able to get on with their three essential tasks, building the fort, the first requisite of all European settlements in the New World; erecting huts for accommodation; and preparing the nearby land for the spring sowing. The one thing they did not lack was meat and fish. John White mentions the deer which were feeding on the melons within the confines of the previous fort. He also painted pictures of Indians fishing with spears and nets and shows the sea abounding in whales and dolphins. As for fruits and vegetables, we have a detailed contemporary account left us by Thomas Hariot, the mathematician, surveyor, and scientific observer. Hariot had gone to Virginia with the expedition of 1585, staying for a whole year exploring and making notes on the products of this new world. Two of the plants he brought back with him to England later became known as *tobacco* and *potato*. His findings were published under the title of *A Briefe and True Report of the New Found Land of Virginia*; and it is from this book that we learn of the edible plants as grown by the Indians. They include maize, beans, peas, pumpkins, melons, grapes, and various herbs for seasoning soup. The soil, moreover, was so fertile that no manuring was necessary and no particular preparation required with plough or harrow. Hariot concludes that: 'one man may prepare and cultivate as much ground with less than twenty four hours of labour as will supply him food in abundance for a year.'[1]

1. *The New World, op cit*, pp 245–6.

In view of this superabundance of food and the apparent security of the surrounding countryside, the mystery of the abandonment of the City of Raleigh and the disappearance of the colonists is all the more perplexing.

Governor White, back in England, for the next three years struggled in vain to organize relief ships for the stranded colony. And as for these 114 Englishmen and women (with what new children had been born after White's leaving), we know that they did complete the building of the fort, and we can assume that for a time they lived in peace with the Indians. At this point we have to fall back on the occasional reports of visiting seamen and, eventually, on archaeology to learn what we can of the rest of the story.

These are the last references to the City of Raleigh.

First, we have Governor White's personal account of what he found on his return in 1590, three years after the initial settlement. White set out with three ships, the *Hopewell*, *John Evangelist*, and *Little John*, on 20 March 1590. Unfortunately for the colonists, the captains of these vessels were scarcely interested at all in their fate, being far more intent on piratical attacks on the Spanish West Indian fleets, an activity which had now become big business, involving scores of British ships and thousands of seamen. Consequently, instead of sailing direct to Roanoke Island, the *Hopewell*, *John Evangelist*, and *Little John* dodged back and forth between the Florida Channel and the islands of the West Indies, lying in wait for the Havana squadron of the Spanish merchant fleet. Three months were spent in chasing and sometimes capturing ships, some large, some small, but all laden with the riches of the Indies. It was no wonder that both the masters and crews of the relief vessels were loath to leave the Caribbean to go north to Virginia where there would be no more prizes. However, at the beginning of August, a period when the Atlantic gales are imminent, two ships from the fleet did arrive off the Carolina

Banks between Cape Fear and Cape Lookout. They were now further delayed by gale-force winds in very treacherous waters and had great difficulty in finding an inlet into the sound inside the chain of islands. They eventually managed to do so and anchored off Hatarask Island on 15 August, almost six months to the day since they had left Plymouth. Seeing a column of smoke rising from the site of the colony, they were sure that all was well. Governor White now went ashore and walked in the direction where they had seen the smoke, but on arriving at the place found no explanation for the incident, since there was no sign of a human being anywhere in the vicinity. The smoke must have come from a fire lit by the Indians who had quickly retired on seeing the English ships. As it was growing dark, the landing party had to return to the mother-ship.

The next day they tried again, this time with two boats, one of which was overturned and swamped with the loss of seven men, including Captain Spicer, master of one of the vessels. This was a severe blow to the expedition force which was to have repercussions later. But the ships pressed on up Roanoke Sound and were again encouraged by the appearance of a light on the island – 'the light of a great fire through the woods to the which we presently rowed.' They dropped anchor, sounded a trumpet, and began singing all the English songs they knew, hailing, as they hoped, their countrymen on shore.

Now begins the mysterious and ominous climax of the voyage, for going ashore next morning at dawn, they reached the scene of the fire, only to find it was the smouldering of dry grass and rotten trees. Again no sign of life, either of colonists or Indians. Hurrying through the woods to the north-west of the island, to the place where Governor White himself had seen the settlers established in the vicinity of the old fort three years before, he passed a tree on which had been carved 'these fair

Roman letters CRO'. The significance of this sign was perfectly clear to the Governor, for it had been agreed on his leaving that if the colonists decided to remove to a more desirable spot, they should indicate the place to which they were going by carving the name on the trees around the fort; and, most important, they should use the Maltese cross as a code-sign if they were in any danger. There was no Maltese cross either above the letters CRO or above the word CROATOAN carved on a post at the entrance to the fort. The evidence seemed conclusive: the entire group had emigrated to the island of Croatoan (to-day called Ocracoke) which was the tribal territory of Manteo, their Indian friend and protector. This island until recently noted for its wealth of wildfowl and fish is the southernmost part of the Outer Banks and is remembered as the lair of the English pirate Edward Teach, the notorious 'Blackbeard' who was killed here in 1718. Had the colonists of the City of Raleigh emigrated here? And if so, why?

Governor White, though not yet unduly perturbed, was puzzled. He was puzzled in particular why all the houses had not only been taken down, but the materials of which they had been constructed – perhaps brick, lath, and plaster – had disappeared altogether. Looking for some trace of the track they must have taken to the water's edge, he found no sign of their boats. In brief, all that remained of the colony were some heavy objects like iron bars, pigs of lead, and so forth, and buried in a trench five chests containing, in bad condition, most of the governor's personal effects – that is, his pictures, maps, books, and armour. He had no doubt that as soon as the colonists had left, the Indians had appeared on the scene, sorted over the debris, dug up the chests, and scattered the contents about as worthless.

Still, there was every reason for optimism, since the cross which was the agreed code to indicate trouble, had not been used. All that remained to be done was to sail down the peninsula to Croatoan (Ocracoke) island to find the lost colony.

And now it was that the obsession for loot on the part of the privateering captains of the rescue fleet resulted in disaster. They had delayed their arrival so long while looking for prizes and by now it was so late in the summer that their ships were in great danger as the weather worsened and they made their ill-timed attempts to navigate the treacherous waters of the Outer Banks. They were unable to get their water-casks aboard and had to abandon them on one of the islands, losing yet another anchor and cable in the process. They were now reduced to a single anchor apiece, and, what was even more ominous, the crew who had earlier lost seven of their ship-mates as a result of trying to land boats through the surf were on the verge of mutiny. It was obvious that there was little hope of wintering in Virginia, and a decision was at once made to sail southwards direct to Puerto Rico, by-passing Croatoan Island altogether. In short, the mission to relieve the colonists was abandoned, and the only concession Gover-nor White could get from the ships' captains was a vague promise to return in the spring: Governor White summarizes the situation in this terse comment: 'The captain and the whole company in the Admiral (i.e. the flagship *Hopewell*, Captain Abraham Cocke) with my earnest petitions thereunto agreed . . . But when we demanded that the master of the *Moonlight*, our consort, would accompany us, they alleged that their weak and leaky ship was not able to continue; wherefore we parted, leaving the *Moonlight* to go directly for England and the Admiral for Trinidad . . .'

But the *Hopewell* never reached Trinidad. Still another storm drove her far to the east and the captain, no doubt secretly glad to be on his way home and to get back to the serious business of privateering, set course for the Azores.

And so it transpired that on 24 October, seven months after three relief ships had set out expressly to find and succour Raleigh's Virginia colony, the flagship with Governor White aboard was back in Plymouth. Was it a wasted voyage? Not in the opinion of the London syndicate (of whom Sir Walter was one of the principal shareholders), for the prizes brought home by the *Hopewell* and the *Moonlight* amounted to some £30,000. Indeed, so lucrative now was the business of piracy, that nobody seemed prepared any longer to spend further time or money in searching for the lost colony.

Thus the chances of discovering what precisely had happened to this little community set down on an island 3,000 miles from home were virtually lost; and while the rest of their story is not exactly silence, it will never now be told in its entirety – the authentic clues left us being too few and far between.

Some leads are found in the letters and depositions of the Spanish governors of Florida and Cuba, for while the English seem to all intents and purposes to have abandoned Roanoke and the City of Raleigh after 1590, the Spanish continued diligently to search for the colony and even as late as 1600 proposed to invade it with a fleet of warships and 1,000 professional soldiers. They proposed to do so not for humanitarian reasons, but because English settlements on the coasts of North America threatened their sea routes between the Indies and Spain. However, by this time, the Spaniards themselves were beginning to lose interest in North America, and nothing came of the plan, and after 1602 there are no more references to the English bases in Jacán, as the Spaniards called Virginia. Nor did the British privateers who must surely have called at the Carolina anchorages in search of water report anything at all, and one could say that by 1605 the City of Raleigh had not only disappeared from the map, but also from the official records. The city merchants who financed overseas settlements were now committed to new attempts at colonization – first at Jamestown, Virginia, where 105 'planters' were landed in 1607 and then at Plymouth, Massachusetts, the site of the Pilgrims' venture. The Jamestown Virginians were understandably curious about their predecessors and actually sent out a small search party in 1608, but without success. Forty-two years later, when the Virginia colony was finally well established, Governor Sir George Yeardley reported that four men had visited Roanoke and had been shown the fort by the local Indians. It was seen again by travellers in the eighteenth century, one of whom, John Lawson, mentions 'a find of coins, a brass gun, a powder horn, and one small quarter-deck gun', which only adds to the mystery, since John White who visited and examined the abandoned 'Cittie' in 1590 found no such relics of the colony. Certainly by 1850 only slight traces of the fort were visible and a few years later, when the first serious attempt to identify the site was made, the historian Edward Bruce reported that the whole area was overgrown with pine trees, live oaks, and vines. All that remained above ground was a fragment or two of stone and brick and the faint traces of the circumambient ditch. Not until 1947 was the site scientifically investigated by professional archaeologists who after three years of painstaking work were able to reconstruct the fort, which can now be visited and studied *in situ* by tourists. A few Elizabethan artefacts were found during the excavations, but the site had been dug over so often by Indians and later by soldiers during the Civil War that nothing of any value was found.

The historians and archaeologists, then, are quite certain that they have found the citadel of the City of Raleigh. But where, they ask, were the houses built by the settlers of the first colony (1585–6) and added to by those of the second (1587–

1590)? True, we do not know how many houses there were, except for one, presumably the Governor's house, which had been erected inside the fort. But taking the New England colony of Sabino or Popham Beach founded in 1607 as typical of English overseas settlements, we can assume that a storehouse, church, and a score or more of simple dwellings were constructed within easy reach of the fort. Even so, the American archaeologists, despite most exhaustive investigations, have been unable to locate this 'City', though the search still goes on.[1]

We now come to the last and strangest chapter in the mystery of the Lost Colony.

In September 1937, a casual tourist claimed to have stumbled upon an oblong stone some 14 inches long, 10 inches wide, and $2\frac{1}{2}$ inches deep. He had found the stone on the east bank of the Chowan River at the western end of Albemarle Sound in North Carolina, approximately fifty miles from Roanoke Island and the site of the City of Raleigh. This distance is important since John White had stated in his *Report of His Last Voyage to Virginia in the Year 1590* that the colonists had decided to move 'fifty miles up into the mainland'. The stone was a rough quartz and had been smoothed evidently in order to serve as the headstone for a grave, for on one side (the smoother of the two) was carved a Latin cross and underneath the legend:

Ananias Dare &
Virginia went hence
Unto Heaven 1591

1. See *Search for the Cittie of Ralegh*, by Jean Carl Harrington, Archaeological Research Series No 6, National Park Service, US Department of the Interior, Washington, 1962, pp 54–5.

Anye Englishman shew
John White Govr Via

On the obverse of the stone was carved a message seventeen
lines long as follows:

  1 Father soone After yov
  2 goe for Englande wee cam
  3 hither onlie misarie & Warre –
  4 two yeere Above halfe DeaDe ere tow
  5 yeere more from sickenes beine fovre & twentie
  6 salvage with message of shipp unto us smal
  7 space of time they affrite of revenge rann
  8 al alwaye wee bleeve yt nott yov soon after
  9 ye salvages faine spirts angrie suddaine
10 murther al save seaven mine childe –
11 ananias to slaine with mvch misarie –
12 bvrie al neere fovre myles easte this river
13 vppon smal hil names writ al ther
14 on rocke putt this there alsoe salvage
15 shew this vnto yov & hither wee
16 promise yov to give greate
17 plentie presents
              EWD

Modernized, this message reads:

Father, soon after you set out for England, we removed to
this place. For two years we suffered only distress and war.
After another two years over half of us were dead, twenty-
four dying from disease. A savage [i.e., an Indian] came to
us with news of the arrival of a ship, but after a little while
they [the savages] being terrified of revenge, all ran away.
We believed the ship was not yours. The savages pretended

that the spirits were angry and suddenly murdered every-body except seven people. My child [Virginia] and Ananias [Dare] were slain with much distress. All the dead were buried some four miles east of this river [the Chowan] upon a small hill, and all their names inscribed on a rock. [I intend] to put this message there as well. If a savage shows this stone to you, we have promised that you will give him many valuable gifts.

E(linor) W(hite) D(are)

The implication of this remarkable artefact was that it must either have been inscribed by one of the original colonists, or by a twentieth-century impostor with a first-class knowledge not only of Tudor history but also of Elizabethan vernacular. For both the facts and the phraseology are right. As regards the former, William Strachey, secretary to the Jamestown colonists, reports around 1612 that the Indian chief Powhatan at the instigation of his priests ('the savages pretended that the spirits were angry') massacred all the surviving colonists save seven, four men, two boys and a girl ('suddenly murdered everybody except seven people'). These seven lived under the protection of a chief called Eyanoco on the Chowan River. (This is where the Dare stone was found.) Further, Governor White's relief ship, the *Hopewell*, did anchor off Roanoke Island ('a savage came to us with news of the arrival of a ship'), and it was certainly probable that the Indians, in view of their hostility towards the colonists and their looting of the settle-ment, would 'all run away'. Finally, the remaining colonists might well have believed the ship reported by the Indians was Spanish, not English, especially since it stayed for only a day or so in the vicinity.

As for the language, apart from one or two words, or the forms in which they appear, both usage and spelling are creditably Elizabethan. The expression 'goe for Englande', for instance, could only have been employed by someone who was familiar with it from general usage or, alternatively, knew it as a student of Tudor English. 'To go(e) for a place' has the precise meaning of 'to set out by ship, to embark' and appears in Elizabethan journals only in this sense – as *The Lord Roos has gone for Spain*. So, too, 'sudden (*suddaine* in the text of the Stone) was used in that time as an adverb: Spenser, writing in 1590, speaks of: 'The day with cloudes was suddeine overcast.' Elizabethan spelling was, of course, quasi-phonetical and therefore erratic, whence the language and spelling of the Stone, if authentic, would in view of the level of education and literacy of the colonists tend to be crude.

But having said this, one cannot free one's mind from certain stubborn doubts, particularly as the production of inscribed stones by impostors has been a frequent occurrence in the United States. Thus, more than a score of rocks from the Atlantic to the Pacific have been credited with bearing runic inscriptions of the Vinland period, two of the most famous being one found in Minnesota and purporting to commemorate a Scandinavian expedition of 1362; and another found in Massachusetts actually bearing the name of Leif Eriksson. The controversy surrounding these Norse or Runic Stones still continues.

The professors at Emory University, North Carolina, where the Stone was first brought by its finder in 1937, were non-committal, despite an exhaustive investigation. They were also unwilling to reveal the name of the finder and the exact location where the Stone was unearthed. Since that time, the artefact has not figured at all in historical or archaeological treatises concerning the City of Raleigh and the lost Colony. Perhaps the silence speaks for itself.

What, then, do we know of the provenance of the Dare Stone?

In the summer of 1937, President Franklin D. Roosevelt

had suggested that a pageant commemorating the founding of the City of Raleigh be staged in a specially built arena on the original site of the Lost Colony. A Mr Harrington, who was commissioned to organize this historic festival, was approached during the course of his preparations by a man he describes as 'remarkably like pictures of a Kentucky colonel . . . grey hair, a goatee, friendly, and exceedingly well-educated'. This visitor was carrying two suitcases from each of which he produced an inscribed stone purporting to relate to the Lost Colony. Discoursing on the importance of these artefacts, he suggested to Mr Harrington that the stone with the long inscription (the text given on p 183), be fortuitously 'discovered' while the workmen were excavating the arena where the pageant was to be performed. The resulting publicity, he suggested, would be phenomenal. Mr Harrington declined the offer.

The 'Kentucky colonel' now hastily withdrew and was never heard of again. He had evidently disposed of his relics by throwing them out of his car on to the bank of the Chowan River where they were subsequently found by a Mr L. E. Hammond of California. Mr Hammond, it appears, was looking for hickory nuts when he stumbled across the stones which were now half-buried in the sand; and noting that one of the rocks had a cross on it, he concluded that he had found a marker for the treasure rumoured to have been buried somewhere along the Atlantic Coast by the eighteenth-century pirate Blackbeard. Mr Hammond next appears in Florida, still carrying about his rocks and always hoping to meet somebody who could decipher them. He was advised to get in touch with a university, and next we hear of him is at Emory University, Atlanta, Georgia where a committee of scholars, a historian, a professor of English, and a geologist, made a thorough examination of the Stone and eventually transcribed the inscription. So far nobody was prepared to commit himself as to the genuineness or otherwise of the artefact which the

University wished to retain. Mr Hammond, who had returned to California, was made an offer which he gratefully accepted.

Next, one of the Emory professors most impressed by the Dare Stone, as it was now known, requested people living in the Roanoke region to contact him if they discovered any rocks with writing on them. The response exceeded his expectations, for in the course of the next few months, some thirty or forty rocks, all of them inscribed in fractured English, were delivered to the University; and great, of course, was the excitement among both scholars and laymen. A symposium was held at Emory to discuss the validity of these finds, but no final decision was reached, except by the geologist who, after experimenting with chisel and sand-blasting, came to the conclusion that the Dare Stone had been inscribed by the latter process. Nonetheless, some of the professors of history remained convinced that the Stone was genuine, while others suspended judgement. And so the controversy continued to occupy academic circles until the matter was allowed, as it were, to die a decent death.[1] Once the excitement and controversy had died down, no more stones were forthcoming.

Even so, the mystery of the Lost Colony was bound to deepen as historians made further efforts to unearth scraps of evidence from the archives. It was now discovered that long after Governor White attempted to relieve the settlers in 1590, the search for the City of Raleigh had continued especially in the early years of the Virginia Colony at Jamestown in 1607. The search-parties, though well mounted, never found it and came back from their explorations only with rumours, one of which is reported by Captain John Smith in his *True Relation*: 'Indian chieftains spoke of certain men clothed like me at a place called Ocanahanan'. Another piece of circumstantial

---

1. I am indebted to Professor Emeritus J. G. Lester, Department of Geology, Emory University, for the essential facts as outlined above.

evidence is referred to by Captain Francis Nelson on his 1608 Map of Virginia: 'here remayneth 4 men cloathed that came from Roonock (Roanoke) to Ocanahowan.'

But by the eighteenth century it was obvious that no answer to the mystery of the colonists' disappearance had been found, and the City of Raleigh took on something of the character of legend; and during the nineteenth century vestiges of the settlement had almost disappeared. Now only a few inquisitive travellers ever visited Roanoke Island. Mr Edward C. Bruce, the journalist, writing for the May 1860 edition of *Harpers New Monthly Magazine*, describes his visit to the site of the Lost Colony somewhat in the spirit of an explorer to Darkest Africa.

A short trudge brought us to the site of Master Ralph Layne's stronghold and the City of Raleigh . . . Eighty years ago the remains of a tree were pointed out as that on which the inscription 'Croatan' was found. We could not, however, learn anything of this from the half-dozen residents of the island who were at the fort with us . . . The trench is clearly traceable in a square of about forty yards each way. The ditch is generally two feet deep, though in many places scarcely perceptible. The whole site is overgrown with pine, live oak, vines, and a variety of other plants, high and low. A fragment or two of stone or brick may be discovered in the grass, and then all is told of the existing relics of the City of Raleigh.[1]

Thirty-five years later, the amateur archaeologist Talcott Williams found nothing of significance, and not unnaturally was led to wonder whether the site which he had excavated by

---

1. 'Loungings in the Footprints of the Pioneers', *Harpers New Monthly Magazine*, No CXX (May, 1860) pp 733-5.

sinking thirteen trenches to a depth of from four to nine feet was not another Indian mound.[1] But the written records were too definite to be ignored, and in any case local tradition runs back clearly authenticated to the beginning of the seventeenth century.

In 1893 the site of the fort was purchased on behalf of the Roanoke Colony Memorial Association; and from this time onwards the place, which only a year or so before, had been described as 'practically inaccessible, unmarked and almost unknown' was to become a tourist attraction. An annual festival at which a dramatic pageant entitled *The Lost Colony* is enacted commemorates the founding of British America, but as so often happens with the 'discovery' of lost cities, the magic of the place has been lost. In the days when only the outlines of the old fort were visible among the trees, the visitor had a sense of the ghostly past. To-day, the ghosts have gone, and it is certain that we shall never now know why or where.

1. Talcott Williams, 'Surroundings and Site of Raleigh's Colony', *Annual Report of the American Historical Society for 1895*, Washington, Government Printing Office, 1896, p 59.

Part 5

Europe

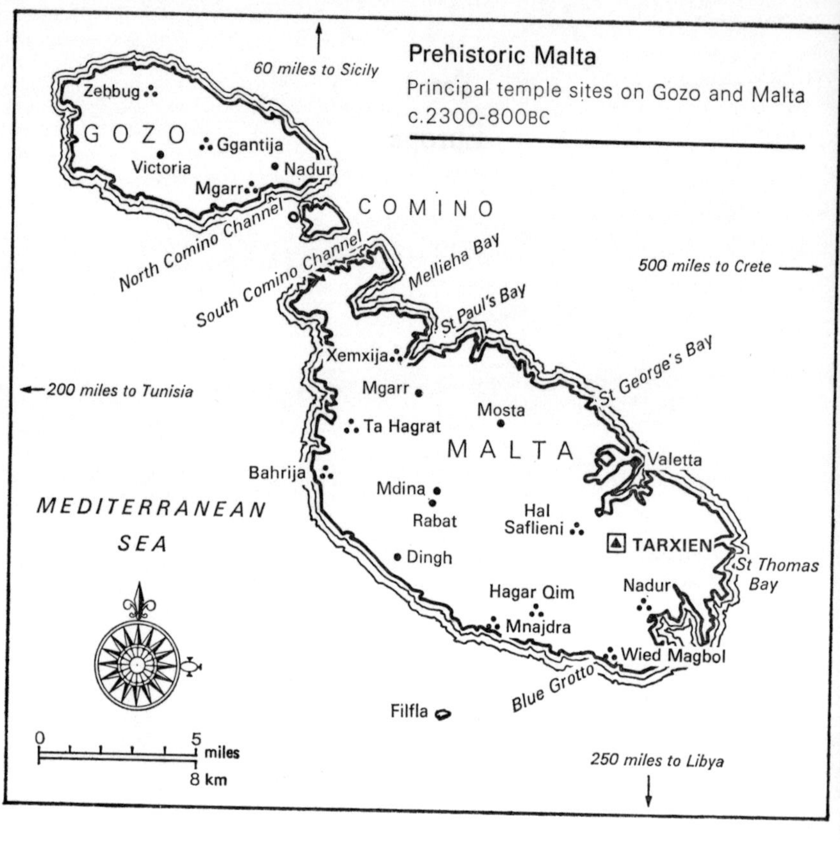

Prehistoric Malta
Principal temple sites on Gozo and Malta
c.2300-800BC
60 miles to Sicily
Zebbug
G O Z O
Ggantija
Victoria
Nadur
Mgarr
North Comino Channel
C O M I N O
South Comino Channel
Mellieha Bay
St Paul's Bay
500 miles to Crete
Xemxija
St George's Bay
200 miles to Tunisia
Mgarr
Mosta
Ta Hagrat
M A L T A
Bahrija
Valetta
Mdina
Hal
Saflieni
Rabat
TARXIEN
MEDITERRANEAN
SEA
Dingh
St Thomas
Bay
Nadur
Hagar Qim
Mnajdra
Wied Magbol
Blue Grotto
Filfla
0
5 miles
8 km
250 miles to Libya

An aerial view of Calleva Atrebatum (Silchester) reveals the Roman street plan beneath the crops on the good farming land near Reading. Once it was a bustling, well-organized part of the vast Roman Empire

Many artefacts from Calleva were
lost during haphazard pre-nineteenth-
century excavations: this bronze
statuette of a flute-player was
preserved, and is in the Museum
at Reading

The Calleva Stone:
fragments of an inscription
which include the word
'Calleva', thus authori-
tatively linking Roman
Calleva with Silchester

Tarxien

The temple at Tarxien – and for that matter the other twenty-nine prehistoric temples of the Maltese islands – exemplify the extraordinary difficulties and confusions inherent in the study of Stone Age man. It is no wonder that this area of human activity has become something of a snare for professional historians and even more dangerous ground for enthusiastic amateurs. A glance at the literature on Stonehenge, Tarxien's contemporary, will explain why.

And Stonehenge is particularly relevant to our journey into the past, since not only was the great British monument being erected about the same time as the Maltese temples, but according to some authorities it was built for the same purpose and possibly by the same race of builders. In fact, comparable megaliths in the form of temples, burial chambers, dolmens, cromlechs, and stone circles were being set up throughout Western Europe during the entire neolithic period – from the fourth to the first millennium BC. Yet despite the thousands of examples of this ancient builders' art that survive and notwithstanding the extensive literature on the subject, we are still in the dark as to who designed these monuments, why they were erected, and how they were built; and this is true even of Stonehenge which has been excavated, re-excavated, surveyed, and studied in more detail than any other monument in Europe.

We start with a fact which is indisputable: the size and construction of these imposing monuments prove that their builders were not what the Greeks would have called barbarians. They were a people who had learnt how to live and work together as a homogeneous social group – in other words, as a nation. It was, then, a sense of nationality which unified them, and it follows that there must have been some common force, some shared conviction, which compelled them to devote so much of their time and effort to dragging heavy stones great distances and to erecting them according to some recognizable architectural principle. This seems to have been the same religious force which animated all classes of society during the Middle Ages – nobles and commoners, clergy and people – to toil voluntarily as labourers in the erection of the great cathedrals. It is, of course, a force which no longer inspires nations except, perhaps, in times of war.

But even if the nationhood of the Tarxien builders is accepted as self-evident, very little else about this Stone Age people can be taken for granted, particularly their motives for erecting so many temples at such a cost in time and energy. The most bizarre theories tend to be the most popular. So we have Stonehenge portrayed as a Temple of the Druids, with human sacrifices marking the opening and closing of the seasons. Tourists are shown the 'Slaughter Stone' at the base of the Heel Stone over which the midsummer sun is said to rise. The great Irish megaliths, like New Grange on the Bend of the Boyne, are ascribed to the 'little people' whose homes the monuments were supposed to be. Tarxien in Maltese lore was thought to be the work of giants, especially in view of the wholly inexplicable 'cart-tracks' which are associated with the building of the temple. To peasants whose tectonic skill is limited to erecting one-storied huts, the very size of the lintel stones used in the Tarxien temple indicated the work of superhumans.

The prehistorian to-day naturally pooh-poohs these folk tales as nonsense, and he is equally hard on the amateurs who, particularly in the case of Stonehenge, periodically present a brand-new theory – usually these days an astronomical one.

But having disposed of the opposition, as it were, the professionals permit themselves considerable latitude in their own interpretation of the known facts; and nearly all of them start with the assumption that the megalith-builders of the western Mediterranean – Spain, Portugal, Malta – belonged to the same stock as the folk who built the stone monuments of Brittany, Britain, Ireland, Scotland, and the Orkney Islands. This theory necessitates the supposition that the builders migrated both by land and by sea somewhere in the fourth millennium BC; and while such a migration sounds plausible enough, we are still not told how these Stone Age people travelled in sufficient numbers to set up colonies throughout northern Europe and, even more fundamentally, *why* they should have left their original home and journeyed into the unknown – especially to inhospitable lands like the far north of Ancient Britain.

We shall see how such questions bedevil the subject of Tarxien when we come to discuss the numbers and provenance of the workers required to build this and the other twenty-nine temples of the Maltese archipelago. In short, what was the population of Malta in 2000 BC? Where did the inhabitants come from? And where did the temple-builders acquire their advanced technical skills? To these questions we must add a fourth. How did the Maltese find time to erect so many temples, construct sufficient homes, and grow enough food to feed themselves with the labour force available on such a small island? One has only to see how time-consuming it is in barren countries to produce a crop at all and how exacting the peasant-farmer's life is to wonder what sort of society was able to organize such projects without the vast army of slaves who were forced to build the Egyptian, Babylonian, and Roman monuments. Then again, one has only to examine the carving in high relief in the courtyard of the western temple at Tarxien to ask how such artistic work was accomplished with the crude tools available to the sculptors of those days, all the more so since the island is totally lacking in flints and other hard stones suitable for cutting and dressing stone.

It used to be difficult to answer these questions because of the traditional concept of Stone Age man as a hairy cave-dweller, ape-like in intellect as well as appearance, and incapable of doing much more than drag back his kill to the cave wherein he dwelt. For this reason the International Anthropological Congress which met in Barcelona in 1880 and heard a report of the wall paintings in the newly discovered Altamira caves suspected a hoax and even when assured that the murals were genuine refused to believe that they could be the work of palaeolithic artists. To-day, however, the pendulum of what might be called anthropological fashion has swung so far the other way that certain prehistorians ask us to believe that our Western European ancestors were highly cultivated and sophisticated folk; that their scientific and technological knowledge was extremely advanced; and that they built their monuments as astronomical observatories. Indeed, one writer of this new school suggests that Stonehenge was built by Jason and the Argonauts; that Britain of the second millennium BC was the Land of the Golden Fleece; and that when the monument was finished, the British king put on a plate of gold on his breast, a cape of gold on his shoulders, a helmet of bronze with nodding plumes on his head, and thereupon made a sacrifice to the warrior-god of the sky.[1]

Conservative historians and archaeologists, mindful of the ridicule that awaits the unwary and too imaginative speculator, draw the line at this sort of nonsense and keep to the plain facts – the size and weight of the stones used in the construction of the monuments and the characteristics of the artefacts unearthed during excavations. In the case of Tarxien, the archaeologists and historians were lucky, since the site had

1. See Patrick Crampton, *Stonehenge of the Kings. A People Appear*, John Baker: London, 1967.

neither been looted nor dug over in recent times for obvious reasons: first, Stone Age monuments yield little of value to looters; and second, the ruins lay under a field which produced a rich crop of wheat – and wheat was far more important to the Maltese than the occasional potsherds which were thrown up by the plough. Indeed, it was only in 1913 when the local farmer saw how much interest there was in the excavations of the nearby Hypogeum of Hal Saflieni that he apprised Dr Themistocles Zammit, the director of excavations, of what he was finding in his wheat field at Tarxien.

The first trench was cut at Tarxien in July 1915, and within a few days it was clear that the excavators had discovered another splendid prehistoric temple, this find having all the appearance of being undisturbed. The site had obviously been occupied by the Carthaginians who occupied the island in the eighth century BC and, characteristically, left behind as souvenirs of their occupation a few valueless artefacts. The Phoenicians and Carthaginians were not an artistic people and never seem to have bothered to produce works of art of their own; nor would one expect a seafaring nation almost wholly engaged in maritime trade to spend much time on the refinements which were so much part and parcel of Greek culture. Thus the only evidence of the Punic occupation of Malta (from around 800 BC – 218 BC when the Romans captured it) are their rock tombs and at Tarxien a few sherds and amulets found near skeletons, indicating that the Carthaginians had used the site as a burial ground and, for all we know, had adapted the old temple for their own religious ceremonies and the worship of Baal Hammon.

The layer beneath the Carthaginian stratum belonged to the Bronze Age and consisted of a mass of clay urns smashed into small fragments. The presence of burnt human bones which may have been deposited in these urns indicated that this was a cemetery as well as a crematorium. Also, the finding of various metal objects made of copper, a thin sheet of silver, and a piece of lead proved conclusively that an early Bronze Age people had occupied the site of the Tarxien temples after displacing the aboriginal builders. Where these newcomers came from is not known, but the guess is from Sicily, across the sea less than 100 miles to the north. Nor do we know whether they came as invaders and whether they annihilated or enslaved the native population.

Finally in 1919 Themistocles Zammit reached the lowest stratum and uncovered the three temples which the visitor sees to-day. One enters the sacred precincts by an entrance to the semicircular forecourt and stands where Stone Age man stood some 4,000 years ago and sees the ruins of the very same temple, a marvel of Stone Age architecture, far superior in concept and workmanship to any other neolithic monument in the world, Stonehenge included. While it is not absolutely certain that this and the two adjoining structures were religious buildings, it is difficult to see what else they could have been, especially since carefully sited stones resembling altars or shrines are found throughout the buildings together with the charred bones of animals thought to have been sacrificed on or before the altars. At the same time, such elaborate building complexes undoubtedly served a variety of needs – as temples, monasteries, festival sites, community centres, and hostels for pilgrims. Tarxien, then, was a busy place, thronged with sightseers as well as pilgrims. So much we can take for granted, though we have no idea who were the deities the people came to worship.

The ultimate mystery of Tarxien is, of course, why and how the population of an island less than 100 square miles in area built so many temples. The answer to the first part of this question – why? – can at least be guessed at by making a comparison with two of our other lost cities – Angkor and Copán; and even nearer to Tarxien in time and place, Sumer and other nations of proto-history. All these city-states were ruled over by god-kings; all were theocracies; all were temple-builders. The church, in other words, was the government, and all activities, political, economic, and social, were subject to its jurisdiction. In every case of a theocracy, whether ancient or modern, the hierarchy decreed that the wealth and energy of the nation were to be used for the erection of earthly homes for the gods: no other buildings on this scale were ever erected, not even palaces, since the god-king and his priest-courtiers were housed within the temple itself. Moreover, the common people accepted this theocentric system not necessarily out of fear or ignorance, but with awe and wonder, for there were no other distractions to occupy them, no other spectacles to compare with these huge stone structures from which rose the smoke of sacrifices and the sounds of worship. It does not take much imagination to share the emotions of a prehistoric shepherd who had lived all his life in a hut on first beholding the great temple of Tarxien.

So much we can take for granted. What cannot be so easily assumed is how the islanders, whatever their numbers, found enough workers to build such elaborate structures; where they acquired the skill necessary for dressing and sculpting stone; and how they paid for the project. It is not suggested of, course, that the workers received a wage. But all had to be fed, and if the men were not in the fields, who was terracing the hillsides, who growing the crops, and who bringing in the harvest?

Various theories have been formulated to explain this puzzle. Firstly, the temples are so numerous and imposing for islands the size of Malta and Gozo that the whole archipelago, it is argued, may have become a Holy Land whose shrines attracted a constant stream of pilgrims, as shrines all over the world have always done and will continue to do. The most obvious example to-day is Mecca whose sanctification after the Prophet's death made what was formerly a caravan station on the Incense Road the capital of the Islamic world. So in view of the example of Mecca and, for that matter, of many celebrated Christian shrines, it is easy enough to envisage a society in which everybody, including the attendants of the sacred places, was able to live off the thank-offerings of the pilgrims, just as to-day whole towns live off the proceeds of tourism. But this theory, however plausible it may sound in the context of, say, Mohammedan tombs and Christian shrines, does not solve the problem of Tarxien. For where did the presumed pilgrims come from in 2000 BC? And how did they reach the Maltese islands from the mainland even before the Mediterranean sea-routes were explored and charted by the Phoenicians?

Another theory – once again only an educated guess – is that the islanders financed their building projects by international trade, by exporting textiles, for instance, in return for food. Food, indeed, is the crux of the problem. For the soil of Malta is not particularly fertile, and there is certainly not much of it. Many, if not most, of the patches of farmland have been man-made by generations of smallholders who with the help of their wives and children have humped basketfuls of earth up from the valleys to the terraces on the hillsides. This enormous undertaking must have started in neolithic times, and so we come back again to the mystery of how the hierarchs managed to divert the people away from essential agricultural tasks into labouring on vast public works. How, in other words, were they able to feed them?

There is a possible answer to this question if we compare our modern requirements in respect of food with those of primitive people. Take, for instance, the food consumption of the average well-off English family: we find that the members of such a unit are capable of eating seven meals a day as follows:

1   morning tea with biscuits
2   breakfast (eggs, bacon, toast, jams)
3   elevenses (coffee and biscuits)

4 lunch (two-three courses)
5 tea (tea and cakes)
6 supper (three courses)
7 late-night snack (cocoa or hot milk drink)

Compare this daily intake of food with the diet of, for instance, an Australian aborigine who, in his natural state, is lucky to get one square meal a week. It is then easy to see how primitive men lived and worked on rations which we would regard as a starvation diet.

The dread of hunger must have played an important part in the daily life of the Stone Age builders of Tarxien, and one wonders if the resultant preoccupation with food was not the inspiration for the few anthropomorphic artefacts found in the temple ruins – namely, the remarkable limestone and alabaster figurines of enormously fat women. In other words, are we not seeing here the glorification of obesity, so distasteful to well-fed Westerners, so admired by all under-nourished races? In that case, is it not possible that the steatopygous statuettes found at Tarxien and the other Maltese temples are personifications of the good life in a world in which hunger was a continual tribulation and emaciation the mark of a miserable, poverty-stricken existence? And if obesity symbolized plenty, we have a better understanding of the real significance of that terracotta torso of a female with enormous breasts and buttocks, she who is called the Venus of Malta. True, nineteenth-century anthropologists, evidently embarrassed by the grotesque sexuality of these idols, have confused us by inventing the catch-phrase 'Earth Mother', 'Fertility Rites', and so forth, as if to excuse and, indeed, sanitize sculptures which the artists may well have intended to personify earthly rather than heavenly goddesses. In short, for people condemned to such laborious, restricted, and deprived lives as prehistoric man must have lived the Venus of Malta may have been not a representation of divinity, but a paragon of female beauty, beautiful because her plentitude of flesh typified a plentitude of food.

None of this enables us, of course, to explain why the Maltese temples were built or why their builders should have vanished as if by magic. We are faced with the mystery of the rise and fall of yet another ancient society, a mystery which occupied the attention of the greatest of Greek philosophers in his account of Atlantis, the island-state with so many features in common with prehistoric Malta. And since it is not impossible that Plato himself stopped over at this island on his voyages from Athens to Syracuse in 367 BC and again in 361 BC, he may actually have seen Tarxien and the other temples in their pristine state.

In Plato's day, Malta had been occupied by the Carthaginians – that is to say, the main harbours were in the control of this people who were never particularly interested in colonization. Rather, it was the Greeks who were infiltrating the island culturally, as the coins and inscriptions from this period show. Some of the inscriptions, in fact, point to a special relationship with Syracuse, and it is this connection which suggests the interesting hypothesis that the great philosopher saw the ruins of an ancient civilization and, pondering upon their significance, conceived the fable of Atlantis described in his Dialogues. For Plato, as for all classical philosophers of history, the decline of a civilization was not due merely to physical factors, but to moral decay; and just as he ascribes the destruction of Atlantis to the impiety of the people, so he would have wondered if the collapse of the Maltese temple culture was not due to the people's loss of faith in their gods.

Historians to-day, in contrast, look for more material causes, even though they admit that they see no evidence of collapse as a result of war or invasion. What, then, did happen? Certainly the Tarxien temple-builders can tell us nothing, for not a syllable of anything resembling writing has been found, either in the form of dedicatory inscriptions, or on any of the artefacts unearthed during the excavations. This absence of writing is in itself significant, since by 2000 BC writing, invented in Sumer sometime in the fourth millennium, had spread to Mesopotamia, Egypt, Phoenicia, and Crete. Prehistoric Malta, therefore, seems to have had no intellectual contact with the Eastern Mediterranean, even if some sporadic trading took place. The mystery deepens, for it is inconceivable that a small nation of Late Stone Age people on an island in the middle of a sea should have been able independently to develop a culture as advanced as that represented by Tarxien. And finally, if they were so highly organized as to harness all their resources for the building of some thirty temples where did the people live, and what became of them?

Theoreticians continue to speculate. It is suggested that the end came because of a drastic change in the climate, followed by widespread desiccation, crop failure, and famine. Other theories speak of over-population, malnutrition, and mass emigration. There is not a scrap of evidence for any of these suppositions.

Indeed, the more one examines the available evidence, the more puzzling the prehistory of Malta becomes. In addition to the amazing complex of temples, the archaeologist is confronted with the puzzles of the so-called 'cart-tracks'. These tracks as seen from the air resemble a railway network serving the communities of Malta and Gozo with what looks like the equivalent of junctions and marshalling yards. The tracks are incised in the rocks some 55 inches apart and criss-cross each other at different angles before running off in many directions, some of them actually going right into the sea and others appearing to plunge over cliffs. Nobody has yet been able to explain, or even to date, them. Our only firm chronological fact is that they were there before the first Punic invasions of the island in the eighth century BC.

The assumption, therefore, is that these tracks were the work of the temple-builders who needed 'roads' to transport the heavy stones used in their constructions. If that were definite, they could be dated to around 2000 BC. But the difficulty here is that the tracks do not run to most of the principal temple-complexes, so it is quite certain that they were not specifically made to transport building material. What, then, were they made for? To carry soil from the valleys up to the hillside terraces? No, because the tracks do not run consistently from the valleys to the hills, but wander about along ridges or down in the plains. Yet there *can* be only one logical explanation for such a network: it must have been planned for the same purpose that a road system is built anywhere else – for the transport of goods and for communications between settlements. Self-obvious? No, for anybody who has seen and studied these tracks cannot be at all certain that such was their function: they simply wander and twist about too erratically, and there are too many of them, especially for the needs of a small island whose inhabitants lived within a day's walking distance of each other and whose inter-communal trade could have had little call for a complex freight system. As for the kind of vehicles actually used along these tracks, it is definite that they were not wheeled carts, since the ruts twist and turn too violently. We can, however, deduce on mechanical grounds that a species of slide-car with shafts in front for a draught animal and two poles at the rear to trail along the ground was practicable and would have made the grooves in the shape and depth that we now find them.

But that is all the experts can tell us. The cart-tracks, like the prehistoric monuments, remain a mystery. We see nothing clearly as we peer through the mists of time. The people who built Tarxien are as unknown to us as the god or gods they worshipped.

Chapter 10

Calleva Atrebatum

Choose a sun-filled autumn day to visit this lost city in the heartland of Roman Britain. The leaves should still be on the oaks which grow against the circumambient wall, and the wheat in the fields which now cover the temples, forum, and Christian church should have been gathered in. This is the time of the year when the Wessex landscape looks very much as it did to generations of English folk before us, those who spoke the language of Ancient Britain, those who spoke Latin, Anglo-Saxon, Norman French, and the warm dialects of the yeoman-farmers; in short, all who looked out upon the same hills which rise to the north towards the Chilterns and fall away to the Downs on the south.

But a word of warning! Unfortunately, even on such an English day as this, you will probably have to start your search for Calleva Atrebatum at Reading, and Reading will not put you into the mood for your journey 2,000 years back in time. For this county town which King Alfred defended against the Danes and where the Benedictines built their great abbey, no longer exists. The planners, those meddlesome and faceless bureaucrats of the 1960s, have knocked it down in the name of progress and replaced the homes and houses, even the Tudor mansion of Archbishop Laud, with motor roads, spaghetti junctions, over-passes, under-passes, tower blocks, and con-crete deserts.

So if you arrive by car in Reading, you will undoubtedly get lost, for you must keep whizzing around the maze, without

The main highways of Roman Britain

Calleva Atrebatum was one of the principal road junctions which linked the south and west of Britain with the administrative capital, London

Antonine Wall
CALEDONIA
Hadrian's Wall
NORTH SEA
Isle of Man
IRISH SEA
Anglesey
Eburacum (York)
Mancunium (Manchester)
Lindum (Lincoln)
The Wash
Deva (Chester)
Viroconium (Wroxeter)
MERCIA
EAST ANGLIA
Bravonium (Leintwardine)
Magna (Kenchester)
Watling Street
ESSEX
Camulodunum (Colchester)
Glevum (Gloucester)
Isca (Caerleon)
(Reading) Pontes (Staines)
Londinium (London)
Durovernum (Canterbury)
Rutupiae (Richborough)
Aquae Sulis (Bath)
Calleva Atrebatum (Silchester)
SUSSEX
Venta Belgarum (Winchester)
Regni (Chichester)
Dubrae (Dover)
Isca Dumnoniorum (Exeter)
Durnovaria (Dorchester)
Vectis (Isle of Wight)
Strait of Dover
ENGLISH CHANNEL
0 50 miles
80 km

ever quite knowing where you are or where you are going. You must find a way to escape before you become disheartened and abandon your trip to Calleva. Your best hope is to find that rarest of species in Reading, a pedestrian. With luck, this survivor of an antique age may be able to answer your question: How do I get to Calleva Atrebatum *alias* Silchester? The answer, Take the road to Basingstoke and look out for a sign *To the Roman Remains*.

Let us admit, then, that what with one thing and another, Calleva Atrebatum is a difficult place to find. Even when you get within a stone's throw of the site, it is obvious that casual tourists are not encouraged hereabouts. And rightly so. The land inside as well as outside the city wall is intensively farmed. Cattle are grazed on the earthworks, and every farmer knows what happens to his crops and animals when the 'townies' swarm across his acres. So the signposts are somewhat vague: but eventually you should spot the Wall rearing up through the trees and undergrowth. You have arrived.

Start your tour at the same spot where John Leland, the first to describe the ruins, began his explorations in the reign of Henry VIII, at the farmhouse and church by the East Gate. Both farmhouse and church are still there. If you decide to step inside the Church of St Mary the Virgin, originally and more elegantly called the Church of Our Lady, expect to delay your Roman expedition and to become seduced by the singularities of medieval and Victorian England. The monks from the Benedictine Abbey at Reading who probably built this church somewhere between 1180 and 1200 undoubtedly ransacked the ruins of Calleva for ready-made foundation stones; and when they had erected the sturdy little building that we still see to-day, they amused themselves and those who came to worship here by painting huge red roses all over the walls.

To our delight, the five, six, or seven-petalled roses, later plastered over as pagan emblems by God-fearing parsons, have reappeared thanks to the devoted work of one Miss Ann Ballantyne; and so our eyes wander over the work of some jolly thirteenth-century monk before descending to the chancel screen, a fabulous example of fifteenth-century carving saved from Oliver Cromwell's soldiers after the villagers had removed it and hidden it in a dung heap at the adjacent farm.

Yes, the Church of St Mary the Virgin reminds us, as the fine old Wall of Calleva will do when we sit with our backs against it to have our picnic, that these country nooks and crannies are redolent with the unique quality of the land we know as England. Take, for instance, the register of the rectors of this church. The first is said to have been a certain Morgan, who crowned King Arthur here in AD 519; but that is now admitted to be legend, and we start with the first recorded vicar, John of Knovill who was appointed in 1294. From this time on we have a complete and unbroken list of the rectors until the present, and while many of these worthies are merely names, some appear out of the mists of time as real people – Peter of Gouceaux, 1346–49, who was thrown into Winchester gaol for poaching; Thomas of Lavington, 1349–53, whose brother murdered the curate; Thomas Whistler, 1629–30, who took out the medieval stained-glass from the church windows on hearing of the approach of the Roundheads and hid it so successfully that no one has been able to find it again; Robert Betham, 1698–1719, who lost his thirteen-year-old pupil, Viscount Blessington, by allowing him to be set upon by footpads in London and thrown into the Fleet Ditch and seven years later fell into the same Fleet Ditch himself; John Coles, 1812–65, who upon hearing that the Methodists were to erect a chapel near his church, built the Crown Inn near the site they had just purchased; and finally, a vicar with the right-sounding name for such an exceptional advowson[1], the Reverend and Honourable W. S. Twistleton Wykeham-Fiennes, 1865–80.

Certainly the sun will be going down if the visitor allows himself to become engrossed in the history of this little church and how Rector Peter of Gouceaux managed to get himself caught in the act of poaching ('committing trespass of vert'). So it is time to go out again into the sunshine and to set off along the footpath which starts at the farmhouse and runs right across Calleva from the East to the West Gate. The path is bordered on either side by bramble bushes, and if the season has been good, there are blackberries a-plenty. Fifty years ago, we are told, these bushes and the nettles beneath them, sheltered butterflies that are now so rare as to be considered extinct, which is a pity since they rejoiced in names like the Peacock, the Purple Hair Streak, and the Many-coloured Vanessa. The birds, too, which in John Leland's time flew above these acres are gone, notably the Honey Buzzard, last seen at Calleva in 1879. Collectors were paying £40 for a single Honey Buzzard's egg in that year, which explains why this bird is no longer seen in these parts, along with the Peregrine Falcon and the Green Woodpecker.

We can now get our bearings, as it were, for halfway along the track from the farmhouse, we are in the centre of Calleva Atrebatum, right over the forum, in fact. This forum, now safely tucked away under the fields, covered two acres of the hundred acres of urban buildings which lie within the city wall. It was, then, an unusually large forum for such a relatively small town as Calleva. The plaza, or central courtyard, was 150 feet square with colonnades on three sides and the basilica, or town hall, on the fourth side. All round the courtyard were

---

1. The ecclesiastical term for the right of the presentation of the living, usually held by the lord of the manor, as the advowson of St Mary the Virgin is held by the Dukes of Wellington.

shops and civic offices, so that the whole complex with its columns and porticoes and statues was visible evidence to all Britons that their country was a part of the Roman empire.

The forum tells us, too, why a citizen of Calleva Atrebatum did not think of himself as a Briton, but as a Roman, the co-national of a Frenchman, Spaniard, Italian, or, for that matter, Mauretanian[1]. The Callevan spoke the same language, read the same books, observed the same laws, adopted the same standards, ate the same food, and used the same coinage. There was, of course, one important difference between Calleva of the Atrebates and, say, Lugdunum (Lyons), birthplace of the emperor Claudius. The difference was the relative opulence of the regions of which the British and French cities were the capitals. France, Spain, North Africa, and all the Mediterranean lands were rich provinces, well worth conquering and exploiting. Britain, as Caesar discovered, was a poor country, producing only a few valuable items of international value listed as corn, cattle, hides, slaves, and hounds. Of these only the corn and hides were of much significance, the former to feed the legions, the latter to shelter, clothe, and shoe them. Enormous quantities of leather were needed for infantrymen who marched fifteen miles a day, day in and day out. Italy, France, and Spain, in contrast, were the centres of flourishing industries, international trade, and splendid cities. The industry, trade, and British towns, even London the largest of them, were negligible in comparison, so it is hardly surprising that there is no mention of Calleva Atrebatum in classical literature, and not even the name would have survived had it not been listed as an important road junction in the *Antonine Itinerary*, the Automobile Association Road Map of the Roman Empire.

So even if Calleva had not been deliberately buried by the archaeologists some seventy years ago, we should not expect to find here in the middle of Hampshire a magnificent city like

1. See footnote, p. 14.

Pompeii or Lepcis Magna. There are no triumphal arches, no temples, no columns. What remains above ground, actually only the Wall and the cluttered, overgrown ruins of the amphitheatre, is not very exciting to the casual visitor. The site of the amphitheatre, for instance, is so disturbed that no one has yet even undertaken to excavate it. The city itself, on the other hand, is still there, and it has been meticuously unearthed, examined, and recorded, but just as carefully covered up and returned to its medieval state as agricultural land.

So the tourist who comes expecting to see a British Pompeii will undoubtedly be disappointed and may well wonder where are the marvels of what he has been led to believe is a unique Roman city. Yet Calleva is unique both for the archaeologist and the historian of the Roman Empire. In that case, the visitor will ask, why was such a national treasure hidden away, a question also asked by those critics, eminent scholars among them, who accuse the owners of the land, the Dukes of Wellington, of deliberately denying them access to the ruins? It is a charge the present Duke strenuously refutes by pointing out that the great excavations of 1890–1910 were covered in at the urgent recommendation of the Director of Excavations, Mr G. E. Fox, MA, FSA.

True, there was a time when the amateur archaeologist, or antiquary as he called himself, was able to wander about the ruins and even undertake some personal exploration. For all we know, King John who visited Silchester on 19 May 1215 may have been one of these treasure-seekers, for he may have seen enough of Calleva above ground to give him at least an idea of what life for a town-dweller in Roman Britain was like. John, on the other hand, had weightier matters on his mind than antiquities, for he was about to meet the rebellious barons at Runnymede and to sign the Great Charter on which the liberties of Englishmen were from thence onward guaranteed. In any case, one cannot imagine a man like John who solved his difference with his wife by 'hanging her gallants over her bed' taking much interest in Roman ruins.

The first person to recognize the importance of Calleva was King Henry VIII's official antiquary, John Leland. Henry himself had that strong sense of his nation's history which was to bear fruit during the reign of his daughter Elizabeth. So it was at Henry's behest that Leland set out on a six-year tour through England to make a search for 'the secrets of antiquity'. According to his own account, he visited almost every bay, river, lake, mountain, valley, moor, heath, wood, city, castle, manor house, monastery, and college in the land, and it was his intention to write a description of his findings in fifty books, together with a survey in six books of all the islands adjoining Britain; an account of the nobility in three; and the story of Henry's palaces and castles in five – a total of sixty-four volumes. One is hardly surprised that this ambitious antiquary 'overtaxed his brain', as a biographer puts it, and became incurably insane, but fortunately for historians and archaeologists not before he had at least completed an account of England. It is in his book, the *Itinerary*,[1] that we first hear of the defensive wall which Leland estimated was two miles in circumference, making it a half-mile longer than it is, although he is right about the four main gates. Otherwise he tells us little else about Calleva, except that he was puzzled by the phenomenon of the crop-marks which revealed the street plan. He did not know that the wheat grew more thinly over the lines of paved streets and more lushly over such buried sites as rubbish pits and wells, X-raying, as it were, the skeleton of the buried city.

1. *The Itinerary of John Leland the Antiquary*, edited by Thomas Hearne, MA Oxford, 1744.

The next antiquarian interested in Roman Britain was William Camden who visited Calleva in 1570 some thirty years after John Leland. Camden, rather unkindly described by a contemporary Frenchman as 'a dry-as-dust schoolmaster', was a more thorough researcher than his predecessor. In preparation for his laborious task of writing an eyewitness description of the antiquities of England, Ireland, and Scotland, he taught himself Welsh and Anglo-Saxon so that he could read those native chroniclers whose works still remained in manuscript. After ten years' toil, Camden finished and published his *Britannia* in 1586, one of the first and still one of the greatest contributions to British history.

It is in this book that we read of his exploration of Calleva, which he thought was the Roman Vindomis, a place mentioned on the Roman maps as located on the road from Venta Belgarum (Winchester) to Calleva and identified by archaeologists with various places in Hampshire where Roman remains have been found. Camden must have spent considerable time among the ruins, walking along the walls which, he says, 'remained entire' and actually crawling through a narrow tunnel in order to see the layout of the old city. While on the site he acquired not only many Roman coins and tiles, but a record of the history of the place, tracing the ownership of the estate back to the Norman William de Ow who, Camden tells us, had his eyes and testicles removed on a charge of high treason.[1] But neither Leland nor Camden nor, for that matter, many antiquaries who came after them knew anything worthwhile concerning the history of Calleva, for not even the name of the town was really certain until a commemorative slab actually containing the word *Callevae* was unearthed during the excavations of a temple in 1907.

1. William Camden's description of Calleva can be found in *Britannia: or a Chorographical Description of Great Britain* . . , London: Printed for W. Bowyer, etc, 1772, Vol I, pp 218–19.

In the years before the Silchester Excavation Fund under-took its twenty-year programme of excavating the whole of the Roman town, most 'digs' at the site were of the spade and pickaxe variety, the excavator going vertically down through the ruins in close pursuit of valuable or interesting artefacts. One recalls the early excavations at Pompeii and Herculaneum by means of wells and tunnels and those at the Etruscan sites where tombs were smashed down in order to get at what were regarded as commercial *objets d'art*. The same attitude was characteristic of many digs at Calleva, though the first excavators here were not so much after artefacts – coins, inscriptions, statuettes, jewellery, and the like – as building material. Hence the looting from the Roman city of the marble columns, forty-two of them each twenty-seven feet high, which were dragged away some time in the early Middle Ages, together with an enormous tonnage of bricks, tiling, and dressed stones.

During the eighteenth century there was a resurgence of interest in things Roman, largely due to the publication of Gibbon's *Decline and Fall*, the first volume of which appeared at the beginning of 1776. But even before Gibbon, other historians and antiquarians were studying the ancient sites with the eye, if not the skills, of the modern archaeologist. Such a one was a farmer called John Stair who in addition to his archaeological pursuits acted for a time as the regional cobbler and later as an inn-keeper. Stair excavated at the site of Calleva for some twenty years between 1740 and 1759, and while there can be little doubt that he was after 'curios' and actually dug up 2,000 coins at a site known as 'Silver Hill', he had a genuine antiquarian's interest in the city and a born archaeologist's eye for tell-tale signs. Thus by observing for several years before the harvest how the corn was stunted along parallel lines and how it flourished within the squares marked out by these lines, he was able to draw up a plan of the subterranean city, and his plan published in 1748 is the first, and still an extremely accurate, picture of the street system.

Unfortunately for later and more conscientious archaeologists, John Stair's finds of silver coins and other artefacts went unrecorded, whence much invaluable evidence has been lost – how much can only be guessed at by reports in the local newspapers of what was going on inside the encircling wall of Calleva. We are told that hundreds of coins and other small items were discovered by digging down when the plough struck a pavement and then sifting the earth with a sieve.

This method was sometimes pursued by moonlight, and all the locals took part in the search, disposing of their finds at pretty good prices to the occasional visitor. In one case, an entire mosaic floor was carried off by a gentleman who visited the place.[1]

Reading the list of the artefacts found at the beginning of the nineteenth century and sold for a few shillings to collectors, one can see that Calleva was, in fact, being systematically looted and the finds dispersed, although Stair kept the more unusual items for himself, including a sword with two serpents encircling the hilt, another treasure which has since disappeared. But Stair was at least an intelligent observer and meant eventually to write an account of his excavations in collaboration with the rector of Silchester, the Rev. Robert Betham. Unhappily this parson was the vicar we have already mentioned who ended his career by either being thrown or falling into the Fleet Ditch on his visit to London, and John Stair's report was never written.

Digging of this haphazard variety continued at Calleva throughout the nineteenth century, but already the special

1. *The History and Antiquities of Silchester*, pamphlet published by Samuel Chandler of Basingstoke in 1821, p 19.

importance of the site was recognized by historians. Here, neatly enclosed within its protective wall, lay buried an entire provincial Roman city, and no one knew what its careful excavation would yield. It was now recognized on all sides that the project of completely uncovering Calleva should be undertaken by experts. Work began in 1890 under the aegis of the best archaeologists of the period, among them General Augustus Fox-Pitt-Rivers, the founder of modern archaeological method. Twenty years later Calleva Atrebatum had been almost wholly uncovered: the foundations of a complete provincial Roman city had been revealed. Once the site had been meticulously examined, described, and photographed, the order was given to cover it up again. The acreage of 'good and fat soil' as Camden described it was needed for agriculture and, in any case, the ruins, exposed now to the elements, were beginning to crumble. By 1910 the town of Calleva had once again disappeared from the scene except for its splendid wall.

As the visitor wanders about this little corner of English countryside, circumambulating the city wall and finding a pleasant spot at which to picnic (try the section of the battlements near the South Gate and not far from Onion's Hole through which the antiquary, William Camden crawled to get inside the town), he will admittedly have to make quite a mental effort to see before him the roof and columns of the forum and scattered over the stubbled fields the temples, shops, and houses of the citizens of Calleva Atrebatum. In fact, just in front of him lie the ruins of the town hostelry, an important and busy institution seeing that it served military and commercial travellers from the four points of the compass, notably the traffic of the London and the Bath roads. This *hospitium* had a main courtyard, stables, bedrooms, and its own bathing establishment, furnished with undressing rooms, cold and hot baths, and steam rooms. This hotel, it appears, would have deserved four stars (assuming the restaurant came up to standard) since it had private suites heated by the usual Roman under-the-floor heating system and its own spring water. It undoubtedly accommodated general officers of the legions and their staffs as well as important state functionaries using the imperial post.

Nothing, alas! of this well-appointed inn is now visible, and nothing of the little church, thought to be Christian. It is under the field over there in the south-east corner of the forum, a very small place of worship indeed since it measures only 24 by 42 feet overall and could not have accommodated more than a few dozen celebrants. Christianity had become legalized in Britain by the Edict of Toleration issued in 313, and the Britons seem to have been enthusiastic about this new religion, for evidence of their conversion is found all over the province. Many Christian objects found at Calleva are seals with the Chi-Rho monogram and a ring with the inscription, *May Senicianus live in the Lord.*

Most of the artefacts found during the excavations of 1890 to 1910 are now housed in the Museum at Reading, this delightful Victorian building having, for the time being at least, survived the fury of the planners. The Duke of Wellington has loaned his collection to the Museum, so that the exhibit is as complete as it can be made. The objects on display cannot, of course, be compared with the treasures of the Mediterranean world and the visitor must make allowance for this fact. It must be said at once that many of these Calleva artefacts, while of special interest to the archaeologist, are not very evocative for the layman, nor can the few bits and pieces of carving on display be called aesthetically exceptional. The importance of these exhibits is, of course, the light they throw on the world of the ordinary Roman citizen who lived and worked in a provincial British city some 1,600 years ago. Here in this room ancient history becomes human, whereas in the great museums it tends to remain an academic exercise. Instead of the massive statues of the gods, the busts of the emperors, and reproductions of Greek statues, we see the tools actually used by the carpenters and blacksmiths, the tongs, anvil, file, and hammer, the farrier's rasp, the farmer's sickles and pruning hooks, and the utensils used in a country household, including a spoon with a girl's name scratched on it ('Primania') and the baby's feeding bottle with a rough imitation nipple sprouting from the side.

The Museum artists, advised by the archaeologists, have drawn some splendid imaginative reconstructions of Calleva in its heyday, with detailed pictures of the forum, temples, and the Christian church, and the layman must be grateful to them, for now that even the skeleton of the town has been interred, there is no other way of visualizing what this important provincial centre looked like. One has to take the 1890–1909 Survey reports for granted, and fortunately the team which did the work was composed of dedicated and conscientious archaeologists. They dealt with the facts and on the basis of facts built up a picture of what life was like for the average citizen of Calleva Atrebatum. It was possible to prove that the Romanized Briton in the fourth century AD lived in a comfortable, well-built house, enjoyed peace and security, was well clothed and fed, and enjoyed the amenities of civilized society. He could shop for both home-produced and imported goods; apply to the law courts for justice; indulge in the pleasures of the public baths with their plunge pools, sweating chambers, gymnasium, and social rooms; attend the spectacles in the town's amphitheatre just outside the city walls; and worship in one of the town's various religious edifices dedicated to the international or national gods, including the latest importation from the Near East, Jesus of Nazareth. It is fascinating to compare the life and activities of such a Roman-British citizen of the town of Calleva in AD 300 with those of an English town-dweller of, say, nearby Basingstoke in AD 1980; for while it is obvious that the two types have a common topographical heritage, in many respects they appear to be completely different species, so dissimilar are their language, laws, religions, amusements, and even their food.

The official language of Calleva was, of course, Latin, which was spoken not only by educated persons, but understood, even if only in its 'pidgin' form, by almost everybody who lived under Roman rule. This is not to say that all the citizens of Brito-Roman towns, all the country folk, all the serfs and all the slaves were literate, for education was limited to those who actually needed it. Manual workers, peasants, soldiers, slaves, and the like had no occasion to read or write. On the other hand, some historians suggest that literacy at Calleva was very widely prevalent indeed in view of the number of inscriptions and sundry graffiti unearthed at the site.[1] For all we know, Calleva produced its own writer, as a comparable provincial city – Burdigala or Bordeaux – produced Decimus Magnus Ausonius, a professor of rhetoric and writer of verses which describe life as it was all over rural Europe in the fourth century. Ausonius's long poem entitled *The Moselle* gives us an eye-witness description of a countryman's daily life as it was in Gaul or, for that matter, in Britain, except that the Gauls seemed to have accepted and absorbed Roman civilization much more whole-heartedly than the British, as is shown by the career of Ausonius who actually rose to the highest rank of all as consul in AD 379. No Briton was ever so honoured. Interestingly, Ausonius was known to the British, for a certain Silvius Bonus attacked him, prompting the poet whose wit was not particularly brilliant to exclaim: 'How is it possible for a man to be a Briton and Good at the same time?'

---

1. George C. Boon, *Roman Silchester: the Archaeology of a Romano-British Town*, Max Parrish: London, 1957, p 221, note 4.

It tells us a great deal about the traditional antipathy of the French and English.

No doubt, then, Calleva of the Atrebates, like its Gallic counterpart Burdigala of the Bituriges, could, in its heyday, have produced a writer as competent as Decimus Magnus Ausonius, but evidently its heyday was over by somewhere around the middle of the fifth century when the legions had gone for good and the Saxon invaders had taken over the government of most of Britain. One of the last inscriptions found at Calleva therefore tells a significant story, for it is not written in Latin, but in the Ogham script – a curious form of writing apparently developed in Ireland and based on notches cut against or across a vertical line. Thus the letter B is a simple stroke or bar on the right of this line; the letter C, four bars on the left of the line. The Ogham inscription which was cut on the stump of a Roman pillar found down a well is easily read as *Ebicatus Maqui Muco*: that is, Ebicatus of the clan of Muco. Ebicatus is the latinized form of an Irish name, and it tells us that this man had lived and died in Calleva, but not, of course, what he was doing there so far from home at a time when Britain was being invaded and its Roman cities sacked by barbarians from across the sea. One can only guess that he was a person of some importance, perhaps the captain of a company of Irish mercenaries brought in to defend Calleva during its last days as a Romano-British city.

The town could certainly have afforded to pay well for professional soldiers if the enormous hoards of coins found in and around the settlement are an indication of the wealth of the region. Seven coin-hoards have been recorded at Calleva, giving a total of 12,500 examples of every sort of Roman money. Undoubtedly hundreds, perhaps thousands, of other coins were found or dug up from the time that the city was abandoned. In addition, a hoard of 29,000 coins called *antonin-iani*, first minted by the emperor Caligula and originally worth two *denarii*, or two shillings each, was found alongside the main (Roman) road from Calleva (Silchester) to Noviomagus (Chichester), all this buried treasure indicating the wealth of the Roman Britons and, of course, the troubled times in which they lived once the mighty empire began to break up.

One could hazard a guess that the average resident of a provincial town like Calleva Atrebatum was scarcely aware of this slow but sure decline so long as Hadrian's Wall was manned, the legions were ready to march against any uprising, and the navy was on duty along the Saxon shore. A man could then get up in the morning, go about his business of trading, farming, or manufacture, send his children to school, and leave his wife safely at home to prepare the meals or order a slave girl to do it for her. As Calleva was in all respects a country town, it grew within the Wall a great deal of its own fruit and vegetables, while the fields and pastures just outside supplied all the grain and meat the townspeople wanted. It must have been unusual for anybody, whether rich or poor, to go hungry. The variety of foodstuffs, moreover, was as great, if not greater, than to-day, for in addition to beef, pork, mutton, and kid, the butcher shops offered chicken, duck, game birds, and even stork in abundance, the fishmonger every kind of shell fish, including the much-esteemed Thames oysters. A bizarre proof of how well the Callevans ate is the skull of an elderly citizen complete with teeth worn down to their sockets but not a cavity in any of them. This old gentleman no doubt washed down his roast beef or pheasant with many a draught of foreign or local wines, the former imported chiefly from Italy, Gaul, or Spain, the latter grown in vineyards all over Roman Britain.

Then why did such a prosperous and pleasant community suddenly cease to exist, assuming, as we are entitled to do from the archaeological evidence, that Calleva was not destroyed by invaders, or demolished by some natural disaster?

The answer is that the town did not *suddenly* cease to exist. It decayed in somewhat the same manner that our inner cities are decaying to-day. The inhabitants grew fewer, and in the end those who were left went away. There is evocative evidence of this gradual and eventual complete abandonment of Calleva. In one of the larger and richer mansions excavated in 1895, a house with richly painted walls and mosaic floors, there were found piles of mortar left by the masons, but never used. And then, many years later, somebody had lit a fire right in the middle of the mosaic floor of the main room of the mansion, blackening and cracking the central panel which represented the bust of some divinity or hero. In other words, the great house had fallen into disrepair, it was no longer tenanted, and one evening a lone traveller or wandering herdsman had sought shelter there and had lit a fire to warm himself and to keep away the phantoms of the night.

The squatter's fire is interesting, because otherwise there is no evidence of conflagration and none of wholesale sacking, as one would expect after the departure of the legions and the arrival of the Saxons. In any case, Calleva was not defenceless. The walls still stood, and still stand, built by Roman army engineers to a height of twenty feet and fronted by a ditch 25 to 45 feet wide. The four city gates were still intact with their towers, battlements, and guard rooms. In short, a small, disciplined garrsion could easily have defended the town against a large besieging army, and as far as we know no such army attacked Calleva. The threat to the old civilization and the old way of life must have come from the gradual breakdown of law and order as Roman authority was diminished. By AD 410 most of the imperial representatives – the magistrates, civil servants, and others – had followed the last of the Roman troops in the great exit from the island during the fourth century when the usurper Magnus Maximus denuded the forts of the legions, leaving Britain exposed to continual raids by Irish barbarians, Picts and Scots, and Saxon pirates. As a result, Britain to all intents and purposes became a lost province of the empire; and no evidence of this fact could be plainer than the Byzantine historian Procopius's curious reference to Britain in AD 550, *six hundred years after Caesar's partial conquest,* as 'an island known only by hearsay, containing a wall [i.e., Hadrian's Wall]: east of that wall [he means of course *south,* but along with contemporary geographers, he thought that the British isles were elongated west and east instead of north and south] is a salubrious climate and plenty reigns; to the west of it [i.e. *north*] no one can live because of poisonous snakes and other terrors.'

Procopius was writing of a Britain which had been almost completely conquered by the Saxon invaders. A few Roman Britons were, however, still holding out in the far western provinces, led by a British-born Roman called Ambrosius Aurelianus, said to have been the son of Flavius Claudius Constantinus, the soldier who had been invested with the purple by the legions while serving in Britain. A later historian, Geoffrey of Monmouth, confused this Ambrosius Aurelianus with King Arthur. In actual fact, this whole period of British history – in particular, the sixth century – is really outside the range of recorded history, unless we except a curious tract written by the monk Gildas around the year 540. Called The Ruin of Britain (*De Excidio et Conquestu Britanniae*), this work is basically a diatribe by a man appalled by the weaknesses of his countrymen in the face of the Saxon threat, which was only avoided thanks to the fighting qualities of Britons trained in the tradition of the legions and led by a Roman, called either Ambrosius Aurelianus or Arthur. So successful was this general, particularly at the great battle fought at Mount Badon in which the Saxons were soundly defeated, that southern

Britain at least enjoyed forty years of peace and security. At the same time Gildas implies that the cities, even in those areas where the Roman way of life still obtained, were now only sparsely inhabited. The reason for this is obvious. Town life depended upon trade and a prosperous countryside. With the departure of the legions and the absence of a strong central government, movement between towns, even along the splendid highways which connected every important community in Britain, became hazardous and finally impractical. In other words, it does not need wars to destroy a system. Disdain of authority, neglect of public services, the increase of crime, and the eventual apathy of the hitherto industrious and law-abiding citizens can effect the same end.

This is what seems to have happened to the once-thriving town of Calleva Atrebatum – indeed to all those Romano-British towns which were neither looted nor burnt by the invaders – the Irish coming in from the west, the Scots from the north, and the Saxons from the east and south. The old Romanized families who had been responsible for maintaining the standards as well as the safety and wellbeing of their communities began to feel helpless against the increasing evidence of political and social decline; and when they could, all through the fifth and sixth centuries, they migrated in large numbers to the continent where there were still remnants of the old *civitas* left, despite the chaos caused by the barbarian hordes – Vandals, Goths, and Huns – who were breaking through the enfeebled defences of the empire.

In short, Calleva disappears from history around AD 600 as silently and as unrecorded as when it first appeared around 10 BC as the capital of Tincommius, King of the Atrebates, a Gaulish tribe who had emigrated, for reasons unknown, from their own territories around Arras in France to Sussex in Britain. The Romans civilized these Atrebates, as they did every tribe they conquered, for while we do not know much about the North European nations before the coming of Julius Caesar, we do know from his military records and the histories of Tacitus that all these peoples were, from the Roman point of view, barbarians ruled over by warlords and witch doctors – the former the chieftains of the clans, the latter the priests, or Druids. By AD 121 when the emperor Hadrian visited Britain, not only was the whole island south of the Scottish border in a state of peace and prosperity, but a hundred or more towns like Calleva had been built on the Roman plan, with their forum, basilica, amphitheatre, temples, public baths, shops, workshops, and comfortable centrally heated houses.

The process of civilization had gone even farther: not only were international communications so efficient that a citizen of Calleva could travel without let or hindrance wherever he liked within the known world, but merchants, artists, and scholars could, and did, come from Rome and Athens and even Arabia to trade and teach and perform in Britain. We have their mementoes to prove it. A Syrian merchant called Barates from Palmyra settled on Tyneside, bought a pretty British slave-girl, named her Regina, married her, and when she died, set up a monument showing her with two symbolic possessions, her jewel-box and work-basket, and dedicated her memorial with the words in the Palmyrene language:

REGINA, FREEDWOMAN OF BARATES. ALAS!

Verecunda, an actress, and Lucius, a gladiator, belonging perhaps to a Roman troop, plighted their troth on a fragment of pottery while visiting Leicester. And the Greek lecturer Demetrius who had taught rhetoric in British schools in AD 80–82 dedicated at York a little silver-gilt tablet to the god of the sea and his wife asking for a safe passage home.[1]

1. See Inscriptions 183, 55, and 62 in A. R. Burn, *The Romans in Britain: An Anthology of Inscriptions*, Oxford: Basil Blackwell, 1969.

Such, then, was Roman Britain before the end of the Classical era and the coming of the Dark Ages – a multi-racial society with merchants, soldiers, and professional men from all over the known world. And such a town was Calleva Atrebatum, no doubt with a cosmopolitan population of wine importers from Spain, veteran legionnaires from Syria, and school-masters from Greece, although we have no written records of the people who lived here and no tombstones to give us a hint of their names and provenance. All the same, faint echoes of their voices come down to us, especially on the few potsherds that were thrown on to rubbish dumps. The most interesting example is a broken tile on which a Callevan schoolboy (or so we guess) had begun to write the first line of the Second Book of Virgil's *Aeneid*:

Conticuere omnes intentique ora tenebant . . .[1]

The boy has managed the first two words, *Conticuere omnes*, after which he may have started daydreaming. In any case, whoever he was, he seems never to have finished his exercise and, perhaps, was scolded by his master as an idle boy who would never make a success of anything. Yet he has at least succeeded in making contact with us some sixteen centuries later, for somehow that scrawl on a broken tile, like the *graffiti* of Pompeii, enables those who make the pilgrimage to Calleva Atrebatum to overcome their disbelief and probably their disappointment at finding nothing left of this thriving city but ploughed fields inside a crumbling wall. In a way, that message, 'All fell silent', is the epitaph of all the lost works of men now hidden beneath the soil and especially of those cities we have visited, even if only in imagination, on this journey to some forgotten places.

1. 'All fell silent and fixed their gaze [upon him].'

Bibliography

The following list represents a fairly comprehensive selection of both scholarly books and travellers' tales chosen for readers whose interest may have been sufficiently stimulated to encourage further study of one or more of our ten cities.

I have taken special care to include the narratives of the early explorers which the reader will find marked with an asterisk. Unfortunately these marvellous and rewarding books are now nearly all out of print and will have to be tracked down via the inter-library loan system to the national libraries. They will, however, repay the effort, for these old travellers, especially the Victorians, were the most entertaining as well as the most intelligent observers.

PART I
1 *Sodom and Gomorrah*

ADAMNAN, SAINT, *The Pilgrimage of Arculfus in the Holy Land about the year A.D. 670*, London: Palestine Pilgrims Text Society, Vol 3, 1886.

ALBRIGHT, WILLIAM F., *The Archaeology of Palestine*, London: Pelican Books, No A 199.

*BURCKHARDT, JOHN LEWIS, *Travels in Syria and the Holy Land*, London: Murray, 1822.

CAIGNART DE SAULCY, LOUIS F. J., *La Palestine, le Jourdain, et la Mer-Morte*, Paris: Rouvier, 1854.

CLAPP, F. G., 'The Site of Sodom and Gomorrah', *American Journal of Archaeology*, Vol XL (1925).

HARDING, GERALD W. L., *The Antiquities of Jordan*, London: Lutterworth Press, 1959.

HARLAND, J. P., 'Sodom and Gomorrah', *Biblical Archaeology*, Vols V (1942) and VI (1943).

*IRBY, CHARLES LEONARD and MANGLES, JAMES, *Travels in Egypt, Nubia, Syria, and Asia Minor . . . in 1817 and 1818*, London: Murray, 1868.

KYLE, M. G., *Explorations at Sodom*, London: Robert Scott, 1928.

LARTET, LOUIS, *Exploration Géologique de la Mer Morte*, Paris: Bertrand, 1878.

LUYNES, HONORÉ, DUC DE, *Voyage d'Exploration à la Mer Morte*, Paris: Bertrand, 1871.

*LYNCH, WILLIAM F., *Narrative of the Exploration to the River Jordan and the Dead Sea*, London: Blackwood, 1855.

— *Official Report of the US Expedition to Explore the Dead Sea*, Baltimore: printed by John Murphy & Co, 1852.

MALLON, PÈRE ALEXIS, *Voyage d'Exploration au Sud-est de la Mer Morte*, Rome: Institut Biblique Pontifical, 1924.

*MOLYNEUX, LIEUTENANT WILLIAM, 'Expedition to the Jordan and the Dead Sea', *Journal of the Royal Geographical Society*, Vol 18 (1848).

ROBINSON, EDWARD, SMITH, ELI et al., *Biblical Researches in Palestine . . . in 1838*, London: Murray, 1841.

SEETZEN, ULRICK J., *A Brief Account of . . . the Jordan and the Dead Sea*, Bath: Meyer & Son, 1810.

Tristram, Henry B., *The Land of Moab*, London: Murray, 1873.

VAUX, ROLAND DE, *L'Archéologie et les Manuscrits de la Mer Morte*, Oxford: OUP, 1961.

WALCOTT, SAMUEL, 'The Site of Sodom', *Bibliotheca Sacra*, Vol 25 (1868).

2 *Marib*

ALBRIGHT, F. P., *Archaeological Discoveries in South Arabia*, Baltimore: Johns Hopkins Press, 1958.

*ARNAUD, THOMAS, 'Rélation d'un Voyage à Mareb (Saba) . . . en 1843', *Journal Asiatique*, Série IV, Vols 3, 4, 5 (1845).

— 'Plan du dam de Mareb', *Journal Asiatique*, Série VII, Vol 3 (1847).

*CRUTTENDEN, CHARLES, 'Report of a Journey to Sa'na', *Journal of the Royal Geographical Society*, Vol VIII (1838).

FOSTER, WILLIAM, ed., *The Journal of John Jourdain, 1608–17*, London: Frowde, 1905.

*HALÉVY, JOSEPH, 'Rapport sur une Mission dans le Yemen', *Journal Asiatique*, Série VI, Vol 19.

INGRAMS, W. H., *The Yemen: Iman rulers and revolutions*, London: Murray, 1963.

LARGE, P. S., *Tribes and Tribulations*, London: Hale, 1967.

MACRO, ERIC, *Yemen and the Western World since 1751*, London: Hurst, 1968.

*NIEBUHR, CARSTEN, *Description of Arabia*, Bombay: Selections from the Records, New Series, No 226, 1889.

*PHILBY, H. ST JOHN, *Sheba's Daughters*, London: Methuen, 1939.

— 'The Land of Sheba', *The Geographical Journal*, Vol 92 (1938).

PHILLIPS, WENDELL, *Qataban and Sheba*, London: Gollancz, 1955.

SCOTT, HENRY, *In the High Yemen*, London: Murray, 1947.

PART 2

3 *Mohenjo-Daro*

BURTON, RICHARD FRANCES, *Sind and the Races . . . of the Indus*, London: Allen, 1851.

CUNNINGHAM, ALEXANDER, *Archaeological Survey of India*, Vol 5, Calcutta: the India Office, 1875.

HEVESY, M. G. DE, 'Sur une Écriture Océanienne', *Bulletin de la Société Préhistorique Française*, No 33 (1875).

MACKAY, E. J. H., *Further Excavations at Mohenjo-Daro*, Delhi: Government Printing Office, 1938

— *The Indus Civilization*, London: Dickson & Thompson, 1935.

HUNTER, G. R., *The Script of Harappa and Mohenjo-Daro*, London: Kegan Paul, 1934.

John Brunton's Book (1812–1899), Cambridge: University Press, 1939.

MARSHALL, JOHN H., *Mohenjo-Daro and the Indus Civilization*, London: Probsthain, 1931.

PIGGOTT, STUART, *Prehistoric India*, Pelican Books, No 205.

WADDELL, L. A., *The Indo-Sumerian Seals Deciphered*, London: Luzac, 1925.

WHEELER, R. M. MORTIMER, *The Indus Civilization*, Cambridge: UP, 1953.

— *Mohenjo-Daro*, Karachi: Pakistan Publications Department, 1952.

4 *Angkor*

*BOUILLEVAUX, CHARLES-ÉMILE, *Voyage dans l'Indo-Chine, 1848–56*, Paris: Victor Palme, 1858.

CHOU TA-KUEN, 'Sur les Coûtumes de Camboge', Translated by Paul Pelliot, *Bulletin de l'École Française de l'Extrême Orient*, Tome 2, No 2 (Avril-Juin, 1902).

COEDES, GEORGES, *Angkor: an Introduction*, Hong Kong: OUP, 1963.

*LOTI, PIERRE, *Un Pèlerin d'Angkor*, Paris: Calmann-Levy, 1912.

*MOUHOT, ALEXANDER HENRY, *Travels in the Central Parts of Indo-China ... during 1858–1860*, London: Murray, 1864.

PARMENTIER, HENRI, *Angkor*, Phnom-Penh: Portail, 1960.

PART 3
5 *Garama*

AYOUB, M. S., *Excavations in Germa between 1962 and 1966*, Tripoli: Government Printing Press, 1967.

BOVILL, E. W., *The Golden Trade of the Moors*, Oxford: UP, 1968.

CAPUTO, G. and others, *Il Sahara Italiana*, Rome: Reale Società Geografica Italiana, 1937.

DANIELS, CHARLES, *The Garamantes of Southern Libya*, Stoughton, Wisconsin: The Oleander Press, 1970.

DIOLÉ, PIERRE, *The Most Beautiful Desert of All*, London: Cape, 1956.

IBN KHALDOUN, *Histoires des Berbères*, traduite par M. le baron de Slade, Alger: Imprimerie du Gouvernement, 1852–6.

*OUDNEY, WALTER, 'Excursion Westwards to Mourzouk', from *Narrative of Travels by* Dixon Denham and others, London: Murray, 1836.

WELLARD, JAMES, *The Great Sahara*, London: Hutchinson, 1964.

— *Lost Worlds of Africa*, London: Hutchinson, 1967.

6 Zimbabwe

AXELSON, E., *The Portuguese in Southeast Africa, 1600–1700*, Johannesburg: Kopf, 1960.

BAINES, THOMAS, *Explorations in Southwest Africa* London: Murray, 1864.

*BENT, JAMES T., *The Ruined Cities of Mashonaland*, London: Longmans, 1892.

CATON-THOMPSON, GERTRUDE, *The Zimbabwe Culture*, Oxford: Clarendon, 1931.

COOPER, J. D. O., *The Zulu Aftermath*, Oxford: Clarendon Press, 1966.

HALL, R. N. and NEAL, W. G., *The Ancient Ruins of Rhodesia*, London: Methuen, 1904.

MACIVER, DAVID RANDALL, *Mediaeval Rhodesia*, London: Macmillan, 1906.

POWER, B. F. G., *Zimbabwe Cavalcade*, Johannesburg: Central News Agency, 1950.

ROBINSON, K. S. R., SUMMERS, R., and HALL, RICHARD, *Great Zimbabwe*, Johannesburg: Nelson, 1963.

— *The Khami Ruins*, Salisbury, Rhodesia: Commission for . . . Historic Monuments, 1959.

Royal Geographical Society, *Proceedings*, Vol XIII (February, 1891).

*SCHLICHTER, HEINRICH G., 'Historical Evidence as to the Zimbabwe Ruins', *The Geographical Journal*, February, 1893.

SUMMERS, ROBERT F. H., *Zimbabwe*, Johannesburg: Nelson, 1963.

WIESCHOFF, HEINRICH A., *The Zimbabwe-Monomatapa Culture in South Africa*, Menasha, Wisconsin: University Press, 1941.

PART 4

7 *Copán*

CHAMBERLAIN, ROBERT S., *The Conquest and Colonization of Honduras*, Washington: Carnegie Institution, 1953.

GUSLAP, G. B., *Prehistoric Ruins of Copán, 1891–1895*, Cambridge, Mass: Peabody Museum of Archaeology, Vol 1 No 1 (1896).

LE PLONGEON, AUGUSTUS, *Sacred Mysteries among the Mayas . . . 11,500 Years ago*, New York: Macoy, 1886.

LONGYEAR, J. M., *Copán Ceramics*, Washington: Carnegie Institution, Publication 597 (1952).

*MAUDSLEY, ALFRED PERCIVAL, *Archaeologia Centrali-Americana*, London: Witherby & Co, 1879.

MORLEY, SYLVANUS GRISWOLD, *The Ancient Maya*, London: OUP, 1946.

— *Popol Vuh*, English version by Delia Goetz and S. G. Morley, London: Gollancz, 1951.

*STEPHENS, JOHN LLOYD, *Incidents of Travel in Central America*, New Brunswick: Rutgers University Press, 1949.

STONE, DORIS, *The Archaeology of Central and Southern Honduras*, Cambridge, Mass: Papers of the Peabody Museum of Archaelogy and Ethnology, Harvard University, Vol 49 No 3 (1957).

THOMPSON, J. ERIC, *Rise and Fall of the Maya Civilization*, London: Gollancz, 1956.

VON HAGEN, Victor W., *Maya Explorer*, Norman: University of Oklahoma Press, 1947.

8 *The City of Raleigh*

ANDREWS, CHARLES M., *The Colonial Period of American History*, New Haven: Yale UP, 1964.

*BURRAGE, HENRY S., *Early English and French Voyages*, (Original Narratives of Early American History), New York: Scribners, 1946.

CORBET, JULIAN, *Drake and the Tudor Navy*, London: Longmans Green, 1899.

*DE BRY, THEODORE, *The New World*, NY: Duell Sloan & Pearce, 1946.

GREEN, PAUL, *The Lost Colony*, Chapel Hill: U of North Carolina Press, 1939.

*HAKLUYT, RICHARD, *The Principle Navigations, Voyages, Traffiques, and Discoveries of the English Nation*, London: Dent, 1927–8.

HAMILTON, MCMILLAND, *Sir Walter Raleigh's Lost Colony*, Raleigh, North Carolina: Edwards & Broughton Printing Company, 1907.

BRUCE, EDWARD G., 'Loungings in the Footprints of the Pioneers', *Harpers New Monthly Magazine*, No CXX (May 1860).

HARRINGTON, JEAN CARL, *Search for the Cittie of Raleigh*, Washington: US Department of Interior, Archaeological Research Series, No 6.

PEARCE, HAYWOOD J., 'New Light on the Roanoke Colony', *Journal of Southern History*, Vol 24, No 3 (May 1938).

*QUINN, DAVID BEERS, *The Roanoke Voyages, 1584-90*, London: The Hakluyt Society, 1955.

STITH, WILLIAM, *History of Virginia*, Spartanburg, South Carolina: Reprint Company, 1965 (Virginia Heritage Series, No 3).

WILLIAMSON, TALCOTT, 'Site of Raleigh's Colony', Washington: The American Historical Association, *Annual Report*, 1895.

PART 5
9 *Tarxien*

DENNIS, NIGEL, *Essay on Malta*, London: Murray, 1973.

EVANS, JOHN DAVIES, *Malta*, London: Thames & Hudson 1959.

GRACIE, H. S., 'The Ancient Cart Tracks of Malta', *Antiquity*, Vol 28 (1954).

ZAMMIT, THEMISTOCLES, *Prehistoric Malta: the Tarxien Temple*, London: OUP, 1930.

10 *Calleva Atrebatum*

BOON, G. C., *Roman Silchester*, London: Parrish, 1957.

*CAMDEN, WILLIAM, *Britannia: or a Chorographical Description of Great Britain*, London: printed by W. Bowyer, 1772.

CHARLESWORTH, M. P., *The Lost Province: or, The Worth of Britain*, Cardiff: U of Wales, 1949.

FOORD, EDWARD A., *The Last Age of Roman Britain*, London: Harrap, 1925.

Guide to Silchester, Printed at Basingstoke, 1823.

HAVERFIELD, FREDERICK, *Roman Occupation of Britain*, London: Milford, 1924.

MARGARY, IVAN, *Roman Roads in Britain*, London: John Baker, 1967.

QUENNEL, M. and N. H., *Everyday Life in Roman Britain*, London: Batsford, 1952.

RICHMOND, SIR IAN A., *Roman Britain*, London: Cape, 1963.

Silchester: or 'The Pompeii of Hampshire'. How to get there and What to see, Basingstoke: C. J. Jacob, 1886.

Index